Remote Production:
Your Professional Guide to Cloud-Based Broadcasting, IP Video and Audio

BY PAUL WILLIAM RICHARDS

Copyright © 2024 Paul William Richards

All rights reserved.

ISBN: 9798324090890

DEDICATION

This book is dedicated to remote production teams. When the world needed you most, you stepped forward—often before the technology was ready. Your innovation and dedication have not only kept us connected but have also pushed the boundaries of what is possible in media production. Continue to innovate and impress audiences around the world.

CONTENTS

	Acknowledgments	i
1	Introduction to Remote Production	1
2	The History of Remote Production	Pg 9
3	The Role of IP Video in Remote Production	Pg 20
4	Core Principles and Genre Specific Best Practices	Pg 27
5	Bandwidth and Bitrates	Pg 41
6	Core Components of Remote Production	Pg 46
7	IP Video Production Fundamentals	Pg 71
8	Zoom for Remote Production	Pg 88
9	Networking Basics for Remote Production	Pg 98
10	Optimizing for Bandwidth	Pg 107
11	The NDI Bridge, SRT & vMix in the Cloud	Pg 121
12	Remote Production Workflows and Team Roles	Pg 130
13	Remote Production Software Tools	Pg 150
14	Remote Production Hardware Tools	Pg 177
15	Challenges and Solutions in Remote Production	Pg 192
16	Advanced Topics in Remote Production	Pg 196
17	The Future of Broadcasting	Pg 208

ACKNOWLEDGMENTS

I would like to acknowledge Matthew Davis, our Director of Technology at PTZOptics. His relentless drive and innovative spirit have propelled our team into uncharted territories, particularly in the realm of remote production. Beyond his technical expertise, Matt has enriched our workplace with a shared enthusiasm for the oddities and hobbies that humanize and connect us. His influence resonates not just through our projects but in the spirited bonds we share as a team.

You can follow Matt on LinkedIn here - https://www.linkedin.com/in/technologicalartist/

In the spirit of giving back, I am dedicating all proceeds from all book sales to First Presbyterian Church of West Chester, Pennsylvania. This gesture is a reflection of my gratitude for the community and support I have received. Each purchase contributes directly to our church's efforts in community service and leadership programs. Thank you for supporting this cause alongside me.

Extra Items

- You can download a free PDF version of this book at RemoteProduction.com/book.
- You can receive a Remote Production Certification from taking the online course at https://www.udemy.com/course/remote-production .
- Supporting videos will be available on StreamGeeks YouTube channel.
- Each chapter and accompanying video will be posted as a blog post to provide an interactive experience at RemoteProduction.com.
- Have additional questions? Email me at paul@streamgeeks.us.

Link to the Udemy course where you can receive a certification for course completion.

1 INTRODUCTION TO REMOTE PRODUCTION

Welcome to the fascinating world of remote production, a dynamic and evolving field that is reshaping the landscape of broadcasting and media production. This book can guide you through the many remote production software and hardware options available today. It will also review fundamental concepts and specific technologies that make it possible such as NDI, Dante, SRT, RTMP and many more acronyms with which you will become familiar. Whether you are a seasoned broadcast professional, a media student, or simply a technology enthusiast, this book will provide you with a comprehensive understanding of how modern broadcasting is adapting to the challenges and opportunities of the digital age.

This book is designed to be used in either of two ways; reading it in sequence (chapter order) or using it as more of a reference book; reading any individual chapter or section as you like. This means that you'll notice some necessary duplications, especially in the defining of terms and variations in which details are explored. One important caveat; there's a LOT of information here, but don't let it scare you. Live remote production doesn't have to be overly complex in order to be successful. This book is about providing options for addressing the many different types, sizes, scopes and needs of the productions that you'll encounter.

Pro Tip: Whatever you do and regardless of which tools you select, just be sure to test, test and test again.

My first experience with remote production was a simple one. I was approached by the team at EasyLive (now LiveU Studio) to test out their cloud production software in 2017. The StreamGeeks were a small three person team operating our live show out of West Chester, PA. Once a week, we would use vMix to produce our live stream, learning from our mistakes, and chatting with our online community. Around this time we had just upgraded our studio to NDI. We still relied on SDI for many of the video connections, but we were transitioning to IP and the benefits were exciting. Our producer, Mike, would mix together our audio and video sources using vMix and stream our show to both YouTube and Facebook at the same time. Wow, streaming to two destinations at the same time, incredible right? (I believe this was before restream.io was a thing).

Getting to the point here, EasyLive wanted us to use their cloud-based video production system. It was new to us but it gave us several interesting benefits. The first benefit was a redundant backup in the cloud. If our in-studio stream went down, which it did from time to time, EasyLive would keep the RTMP connection to our content delivery network (CDN) alive. One time I knocked the HDMI connection out of our LiveU Solo on our mobile broadcast. I didn't realize this until 5 minutes later, but at least EasyLive kept our stream alive, so I could get it fixed without losing our audience. The slide below was one of the first compelling reasons I ever found to start producing video in the cloud.

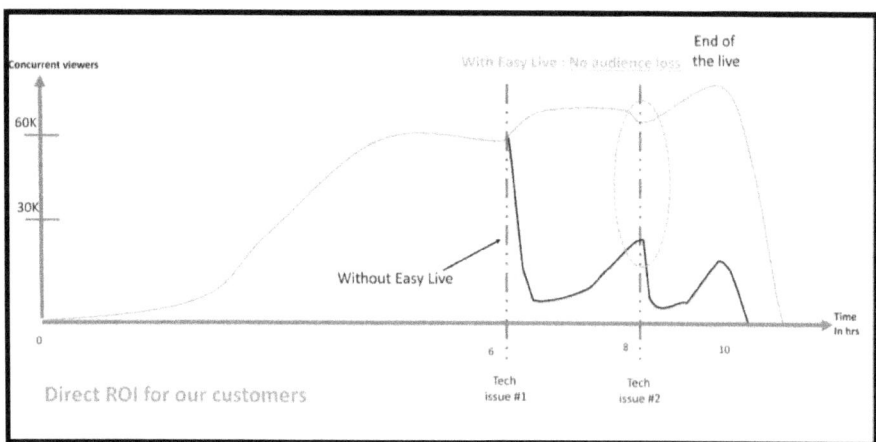

Most live streams will slowly build up an audience over time. When a live stream goes down, most viewers are lost. With cloud redundancy, lost viewership can be avoided in many cases. EasyLive was purchased by LiveU in 2022.

EasyLive allowed us to host an image or a short video that would play when the stream went down. Seeing an image replace the lost video feed was my first realization of the power of cloud-based video production. It didn't take long for us to use the cloud for more than a redundant back-up.

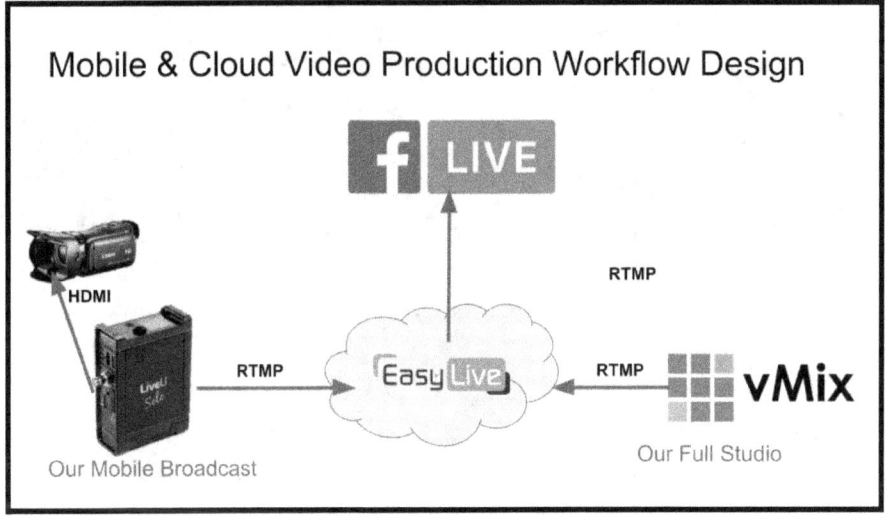

Our first mobile and remote production at StreamGeeks.

In future live streams, we tested mixing together multiple RTMP inputs allowing us to switch back and forth between our in-studio vMix production and a mobile LiveU backpack video feed. These live streams were some of the most interesting to watch and enjoyable experiences of my career. Our audience simply could not believe their eyes when we switched from an "in-studio" production to a mobile broadcast that could walk down the street and hop into a car.

A mobile broadcast using a battery powered LiveU LU600 backpack streaming to EasyLive.

While the StreamGeeks operate on a small scale, in 2019, I was introduced to Ryan Salazar from Broadcast Beat, who showed us how to take things to the next level. At the 2019 National Association of Broadcasters (NAB) show, we got the chance to be part of a large scale remote production. The Broadcast Beat team was tasked with covering interviews from all over the Las Vegas Convention Center. Tess Protesto (my co-host) and I were asked to help host the official NAB show live stream, and it would be the first time we were truly connected to a professional remote production team.

2019 was at the peak of the Broadcast industry before the pandemic.

During the event, we were accompanied by a dedicated video crew, equipped with mobile production technology that would allow us to communicate with the Broadcast Beat studio team in Florida. We used an online intercom system called Unity Intercom which had multiple channels available for the on-site crews to communicate using their smartphones' cellular connections.

Broadcast Beat studio in Fort Lauderdale, Florida, USA.

As on-camera talent, we received in-ear monitors so we could hear the technical director and know when we were going live. Each camera man had a LiveU LU600 backpack sending high quality RTMP video streams back to the Broadcast Beat studio. It was a whirlwind of an experience that still impresses me to this day.

My involvement with remote production technology did not stop there. Through my role as Chief Streaming Officer at PTZOptics, I continued to engage with our team to help build Hive, our remote production software. Hive was designed with a special focus on PTZ camera movement tools. Hive was released at the 2024 NAB Show, and it won Best Product for the remote production category.

PTZOptics Hive showing the joystick tool.

Hive includes some interesting new ways to move robotic cameras which was something we felt the industry needed desperately. Many of the challenges we discovered about remote production over the years, we were able to solve with Hive. For example, Hive features a "Share" button which makes collaborating with others in a virtual video production environment as easy as sharing a Google Doc.

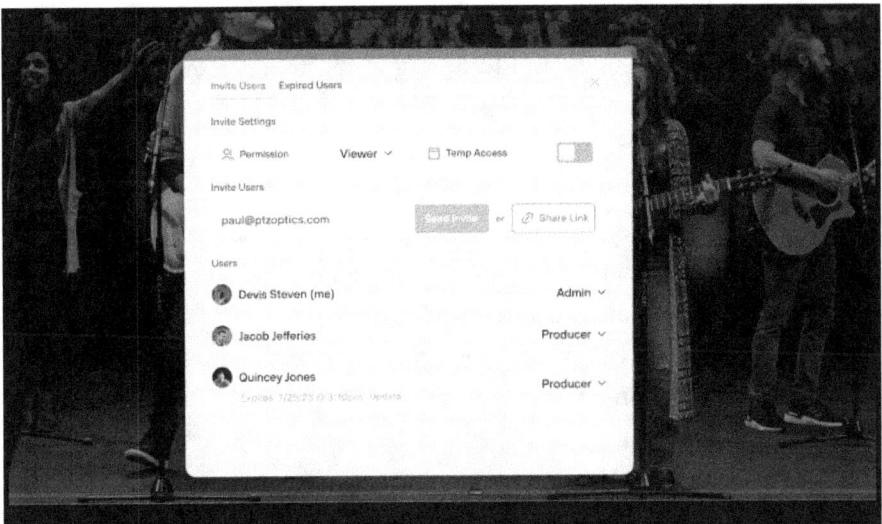

The Hive share module for bringing invited users into a specific studio.

In 2024, 50% of attendees at NAB were first timers. This was apparent in the types of questions people asked and the way the show has shifted in some areas from traditional "Broadcast" to newer "Live Streaming" and "Remote Production" interests. As "Broadcast" becomes more synonymous with high-end television, "Live Streaming" has become aligned with everyday video production for a wide-array of use cases. It's interesting to watch the industry changing before our eyes.

Overview of the Book

This is an advanced book that covers a lot of ground. If you are in the early stages of your education process you may want to check out *The Basics of Live Streaming, The PTZ Camera Operator Handbook, The Unofficial Guide to NDI, The Unofficial Guide to OBS* or *The Unofficial Guide to vMix* which are all available on Amazon. This book is structured to provide a comprehensive exploration of remote production, guiding you from foundational technologies to in-depth information for practical applications. You can also take the accompanying Udemy course and receive a certificate for your education in remote production. This may be a helpful tool in securing work for future remote production jobs such as: remote camera operator, remote color correction specialist, remote video producer and remote graphics management.

How you can benefit from this book:

1. Gain a deep understanding of the technologies and tools that power remote production, including detailed examinations of software and hardware solutions.
2. Learn how to streamline operations and manage remote production projects successfully, enhancing both productivity and product quality.
3. Be inspired by the potential of remote production to transform the broadcasting industry, encouraging forward-thinking approaches to media production.

Growing demand for remote production technical expertise:

There is strong and growing demand for remote production expertise. If you are interested in getting certified for remote production you can take the Udemy course which accompanies this course and includes a certificate.

KEY TAKEAWAYS FROM THIS CHAPTER:

The adoption of remote production has been pivotal in modern broadcasting for several reasons, including:

1. **Efficiency and Cost-Effectiveness**: Remote production reduces the need to send large crews and sets of equipment to event locations, significantly cutting down travel and logistics costs.
2. **Flexibility**: Producers can manage multiple events from a single location, increasing the number of productions that can be handled simultaneously.

3. **Scalability**: As needs fluctuate based on the event size or type, the production setup can scale more readily without the constraints of physical infrastructure in many cases.
4. **Pandemic-Proof:** The need to isolate and participate from home and other locations hasn't stopped creative production pros, including on-camera talent, from creating live content.

2 THE HISTORY OF REMOTE PRODUCTION

Beginning in the 1960s, the concept of remote production took its first substantial steps forward with the introduction of Telstar, the first communication satellite. This satellite enabled the first live transatlantic television broadcasts. For the first time events could be shared in real time across vast distances. As impactful as satellite technology was, it was just the beginning. The development of Internet Protocols (IP) in the mid-1990s, such as Real Time Streaming Protocol (RTSP) and Real-Time Messaging Protocol (RTMP), revolutionized the delivery of audio and video over the internet. These protocols laid the foundational technology that would later enable platforms like YouTube, which introduced live streaming in 2011 and Facebook which introduced live streaming in 2016. It's hard to explain the impact social media has had on the live streaming industry. In 2016, Facebook put the ability to live stream directly into the hands of billions of users via their smartphone app. Together YouTube and Facebook helped to pioneer content creation by allowing individuals worldwide to broadcast content from their living rooms to a global stage.

In 2006, Dante (Digital Audio Network Through Ethernet) was launched by Audinate. This was the very early days of audio over IP. In 2009, cellular networks started to roll out 4G technology, which significantly enhanced mobile broadcasting capabilities by improving internet speeds and reliability. In 2013, Haivision introduced SRT (Secure Reliable Transport) designed to provide high quality and secure video transportation over the public internet. Shortly thereafter in 2015, NewTek introduced NDI, a high-performance standard that allows anyone to use real time, ultra-low latency video using standard networking equipment.

In the mid-2010s, several cloud-based video conference platforms started to emerge. Zoom was founded in 2011, by Eric Yuan, and was officially launched in 2013. Fast-forward a few years and the COVID-19 pandemic put the broadcast industry into super-growth mode. The widespread adoption of remote production techniques, started to take place across the globe. Media companies and broadcasters were compelled to innovate rapidly, leveraging remote production to continue delivering content amidst global lockdowns.

In recent years, the landscape of video production has undergone a profound transformation, driven by advances in technology and changes in consumer behavior. Remote production has emerged as a pivotal development in broadcast, redefining how content is created, managed, and delivered across various industries.

The Business Case for Remote Production

Traditional video production often involves logistical complexities, high costs, significant time investments and travel for nearly everyone involved; especially when coordinating across multiple locations or when dealing with last-minute changes. Remote production mitigates these issues by allowing for centralized control over diverse geographical locations, fewer on-site crew (i.e. camera operators, presenters, etc.), the ability to continue production during pandemics and by enabling real-time adjustments to production workflows.

On-site vs Setup & Breakdown Systems

In the dynamic world of remote production, the choice between on-site installations and on-site temporary setups plays an important role in shaping the operational capabilities and financial efficiency. On-site installations offer a more permanent solution, providing substantial long-term benefits through network-integrated operations that enhance accessibility and simplify staffing. These installations allow for remote operation and monitoring, making them ideal for stable, continuous production environments. On the other hand, on-site temporary setups provide unmatched flexibility and scalability, suitable for events and productions that require rapid deployment and dismantling. This comparison table delves into the nuances of each setup, examining factors such as installation time, costs, flexibility, maintenance, scalability, return on investment, and staff training, providing valuable insights to help broadcasters and production companies make informed decisions based on their specific needs and circumstances.

Category	On-Site Installations	On-Site Temporary Setup
Installation Time	Longer installation time; involves permanent or semi-permanent setup	Quick setup and breakdown; designed for short-term use
Costs	Higher upfront costs due to permanent infrastructure and installation labor	Lower initial costs, but recurring costs can add up if frequently set up and broken down
Flexibility	Can operate equipment anywhere on the LAN with in-house staff. Easy to hire freelancers due to remote production-friendly equipment	Highly flexible; easy to adapt and reconfigure for different events or needs
Technology Integration	Seamless integration with existing on-site tech and infrastructure	Requires independent setups, possibly with integrated, portable solutions (e.g., mobile broadcasting units)
Maintenance	Scheduled and systematic maintenance; remote monitoring ensures equipment is always operational	Frequent setup/breakdown increases maintenance demands and potential for equipment failure

Typical Use Cases	Ideal for permanent studios, educational institutions, and places with continuous production needs	Suited for events, temporary broadcasts, and situations requiring rapid deployment and removal of gear
Scalability	Scalable within the limits of existing installations; expansions require additional construction or adaptation	Easily scalable; additional equipment can be integrated as needed without structural changes
Return on Investment (ROI)	Higher long-term return due to sustained use and stable infrastructure investment	Potential for high immediate returns during active use, though repeated setups can diminish long-term value
Staff Training	Allows for deeper, more comprehensive training on stable configurations; easier transition for freelancers with remote production skills	Quick, adaptable training required; staff must be versatile and capable of handling varied setups

Expanding Possibilities

Remote production opens up new avenues for creativity and market reach. It breaks down geographic barriers, providing access to a global talent pool and enabling the production of content that can be more diverse and inclusive.

One of the most compelling advantages of remote production is its ability to significantly reduce costs and enhance operational efficiency. By minimizing the need for physical infrastructure and on-site personnel, and by streamlining production processes, organizations can achieve substantial savings while maintaining high-quality outputs.

Direct Cost Savings

Remote production drastically reduces several major expenses traditionally associated with video production:

- **Travel and Accommodation**: Eliminating or reducing the need for crew and talent to travel to specific locations cuts down on travel costs and accommodation expenses, which can be substantial, especially for international productions.
- **Physical Infrastructure**: With remote production, the investment in physical studio spaces and the associated maintenance costs can be minimized. Equipment needs are also reduced, as much of the infrastructure can be moved to the cloud or centralized.
- **On-Site Staffing**: Reducing the number of staff needed on location not only lowers direct labor costs but also simplifies logistics and coordination efforts.

Operational Efficiency

Beyond direct cost savings, remote production enhances efficiency across various aspects of the production process:

- **Speed of Setup and Teardown**: Remote production setups are generally quicker to deploy and can be managed from a central location, saving time before and after the actual production.
- **Resource Utilization**: Resources, whether human or technical, can be utilized more effectively. Centralized control allows a smaller team to manage multiple projects simultaneously, optimizing the use of talent and technical equipment.
- **Reduced Redundancy**: By centralizing production activities, redundancies in equipment and staffing across multiple locations can be eliminated, further enhancing cost efficiency.

The cost reduction strategies and efficiency gains offered by remote production are transformative, enabling organizations to produce more content at a lower cost. These savings can be reinvested into creative endeavors or used to price services more competitively, providing a strategic edge in a highly dynamic market. As we continue to explore the benefits of remote production, it becomes clear that its impact extends beyond mere cost savings, influencing broader aspects of production flexibility and scalability.

Broader Access to Talent and Reduction in Geographic Limitations

Remote production not only transforms the technical and economic aspects of video production but also significantly broadens access to global talent and reduces geographic limitations. This expansion of resources is pivotal for creating diverse and innovative content, enhancing the quality and appeal of productions across various genres and markets.

Global Talent Pool Accessibility

The ability to tap into a worldwide talent pool is one of the most significant advantages of remote production:

- **Diverse Expertise**: Remote production setups allow producers to hire the best talent for specific roles, regardless of their location. This access to a diverse range of experts—from directors and editors to special effects artists—can elevate the quality of content.
- **Collaboration Across Borders**: Advanced communication tools and collaborative software enable teams dispersed across the globe to work together in real-time, mirroring the dynamics of a traditional in-studio environment but with greater flexibility and inclusion.

Reduction of Geographic Barriers

Reducing geographic limitations has several key benefits:

- **Wider Coverage**: Remote production enables coverage of events and stories from remote or previously inaccessible locations, significantly expanding the scope of potential content.
- **Cost-Effective Operations:** By reducing the need to send large crews to distant locations, remote production not only cuts costs but also speeds up the production process, allowing for more projects to be undertaken simultaneously.
- **Enhanced Local Representation**: Hiring local crews for regional filming can enhance the authenticity of the content while also adhering to local regulations and cultural nuances.
-**Resilience From Adversity:** The Covid-19 Pandemic, lasting about two years, helped us learn new ways to produce content remotely, often in near total isolation.

By broadening access to talent and reducing geographic barriers, remote production not only enhances the creative possibilities and operational efficiency of productions but also fosters a more inclusive and diverse media landscape.

New Business Opportunities for Video Production Professionals

Remote production not only transforms operational efficiencies and content quality but also opens up a myriad of new business opportunities for video production professionals. These opportunities arise from the ability to provide innovative services, reach underserved markets, and create content that was previously not feasible due to geographic or financial constraints.

Emerging Markets and Services

The adoption of remote production allows professionals to explore previously untapped or underserved markets:

- **Specialized Content Production**: There is growing demand for highly specialized content that caters to niche audiences. Remote production enables professionals to produce this type of content more economically and efficiently.
- **Expanded Client Base**: By reducing the need for physical presence, video production companies can extend their services globally, working with clients from any location. This global reach helps firms diversify their client base and revenue streams.

Innovative Production Services

Remote production technologies enable the introduction of new and innovative services:

- **Virtual Events**: The rise of virtual events across corporate, entertainment, and educational sectors provides significant opportunities for video production professionals to offer new types of services, including virtual event planning, execution, and post-production.
- **Enhanced Post-Production Services**: Cloud-based editing tools allow professionals to offer collaborative post-production services that clients can participate in from anywhere, enhancing customer engagement and satisfaction.

Entrepreneurial Ventures

The flexibility and cost-effectiveness of remote production encourage entrepreneurial ventures by lowering the barriers to entry:

- **Startup Video Production Companies**: Entrepreneurs can start video production companies with minimal initial investment, focusing on remote production setups that require less hardware and can operate with smaller teams.

- **Freelance Opportunities**: Individual professionals can more easily market their skills globally, working as freelancers or consultants for multiple projects without geographical restrictions.

Emerging Areas in Remote Production

Remote production is not only changing traditional business models but also enabling new forms of content creation in areas that were previously overlooked or underserved:

- **Funeral Home Streaming**: Remote production allows funeral homes to offer live streaming services for funerals and memorial services, making these events accessible to those who cannot attend in person. This service has become particularly valuable in providing a sense of closure to families during times when travel or gatherings are restricted.
- **Government Streaming**: Local governments are increasingly utilizing remote production to stream council meetings and public forums, enhancing transparency and civic engagement. This approach allows citizens to participate in governance processes from any location, ensuring greater community involvement.
- **Worship Streaming**: Places of worship have adopted remote production to broadcast services and engage with congregations virtually. This capability has been essential for maintaining community bonds, especially during periods when congregants cannot gather physically.

The wider access to technology and services enabled by remote production is transforming the landscape of video production. This democratization not only empowers a broader spectrum of users to produce and share content but also stimulates innovation in how video production services are offered and consumed. As these technologies continue to evolve and become more integrated into daily operations across various sectors, the potential for creative and inclusive content creation is boundless. This shift not only enhances the capabilities of current producers but also opens the door for new voices and perspectives to be heard in the global media landscape.

KEY TAKEAWAYS FROM THIS CHAPTER:

1. Historical Developments in Remote Production:

    - The inception of remote production can be traced back to the 1960s.

    - The development of internet protocols such as RTSP and RTMP in the mid-1990s further revolutionized remote production by enabling audio and video delivery over the internet.

2. Impact of Social Media and Streaming Platforms:

    - The launch of live streaming services by major social media platforms democratized content creation, allowing individuals to broadcast from anywhere to a global audience.

    - These platforms significantly impacted the live streaming industry by making streaming technology accessible to billions of users worldwide.

3. Technological Advancements in Broadcasting:

    - The introduction of Dante in 2006 marked the early days of audio over IP, enhancing audio network capabilities.

    - The rollout of 4G technology in 2009 improved mobile broadcasting by providing faster and more reliable internet connections.

    - Innovations such as SRT (Secure Reliable Transport) in 2013 by Haivision and NDI (Network Device Interface) in 2015 by NewTek introduced secure, high-quality, and low-latency video streaming over IP networks.

4. Cloud-Based Video Production and the COVID-19 Impact:

- The mid-2010s saw the emergence of several cloud-based video production companies, including the founding and launch of Zoom, which became particularly prominent during the COVID-19 pandemic.

- The pandemic accelerated the adoption of remote production techniques globally as media companies and broadcasters sought innovative ways to continue content delivery during global lockdowns.

3 THE ROLE OF IP VIDEO IN REMOTE PRODUCTION

Networking technologies such as IP (Internet Protocol) have made it feasible to send multiple streams of data simultaneously and bi-directionally. This capability is fundamental to remote production and it has been super-charged by NDI, Dante Video, SMPTE 2110 and other IP video standards which take advantage of this bi-directional connection using meta-data for equipment control, monitoring and status updates.

NDI Overview:

Developed by NewTek and now owned by Vizrt, NDI is a video standard that allows software and hardware to communicate and deliver broadcast-quality video via a standard network. NDI will be reviewed extensively throughout this book as it's truly become an industry standard. It's also a great way to learn IP video with software tools you can download and try at any time on their website https://ndi.video. NDI is an accessible option for a wide range of scenarios, from small-scale productions to educational and corporate live events. It's particularly suited for settings where you want to transmit video over a standard ethernet network (and who doesn't want to do that? :).

SMPTE 2110 Overview:

Contrasting with NDI, SMPTE 2110 is a professional-grade standard that supports uncompressed video and requires a high-bandwidth network infrastructure like 10Gb ethernet or fiber. The advanced capabilities of SMPTE 2110, however, require specialized hardware, complex network setups, and significant technical knowledge, making it less accessible for smaller organizations or those without substantial IT support.

You can learn more about SMPTE 2110 in Chapter 10, Advanced Topics in Remote Production.

Dante AV Overview:

Dante, traditionally renowned for revolutionizing audio networking, has expanded its capabilities to include video through its Dante AV ecosystem. Dante supports interoperability among different manufacturers using the same video codec, seamlessly integrating with the thousands of existing Dante-enabled audio and video products. The introduction of video capabilities allows for independent routing of audio, video, and ancillary channels, providing exceptional control and flexibility in signal routing.

The Dante Certification Program is recognized as a standard for AV networking professionals, providing a clear path for learning about Dante technology and showcasing proficiency to employers and clients. The program includes multiple certification levels and various electives, each offering a comprehensive education on different aspects of Dante.

Dante Certification Level 1:

- Covers basic digital audio and video, networking fundamentals, and setup of a basic Dante network using Dante Controller.
- Suitable for operating a Dante system in daisy chain mode or on a single network switch.

Dante Certification Level 2:

- Focuses on creating larger networks, managing bandwidth, basic optimization, and using external clocks.
- Ideal for systems involving multiple network switches.

Dante Certification Level 3:

- Develops skills for navigating Layer 3 enterprise networks, explains Layer 3 benefits, and demonstrates Dante Domain Manager.
- Useful for building large Dante networks and collaborating with IT staff in large organizations.

Dante Domain Manager Administrator Certification:

- Comprehensive training for deploying and configuring Dante Domain Manager, covering logical segmentation, advanced clocking configurations, user management, and detailed logging.
- Essential for managing large and complex Dante networks.

Dante AV Elective Course:

- An hour-long, on-demand session explaining key concepts of the Dante video platform, "Dante AV."
- Illustrates deployment of Dante video alongside audio and details various Dante AV products like Dante AV Ultra, Dante AV-H, and Dante Studio.

Remote Production

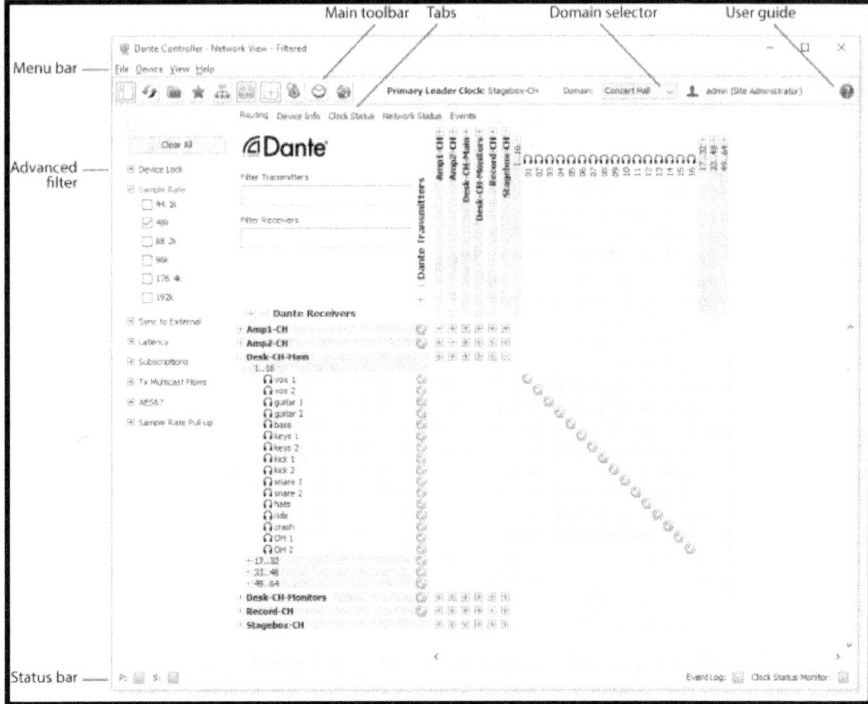

Dante Controller is the primary software tool for routing and configuring Dante audio and video sources.

You can learn more about Dante AV in Chapter 10, Advanced Topics in Remote Production.

Cloud Computing and Software Advancements

The development of cloud computing has further transformed remote production by decentralizing the processing and storage of data. Cloud-based platforms powered by Amazon Web Services (AWS), Google and Microsoft Azure among others, enable production teams to access and route video feeds from any location with an internet connection, providing unprecedented flexibility and scalability. With the computer processing handled in the cloud, simple laptops can be used to perform complicated video production tasks.

While tinkering with these cloud services may seem daunting, there are a slew of services that provide cloud hosting specifically for video production such as V2Cloud. Services like this allow you to quickly build a custom cloud system designed for Open Broadcaster Software (OBS) for example, in just four easy steps. You choose a plan, build a cloud PC, install OBS and get started with your cloud based video production.

Innovations In Remote Production

The technology that we use for live streaming is only getting better with the introduction of 5G technology, AI, and computer vision. 5G specifically is allowing for high quality broadcasts from smartphones giving remote reporting a whole new meaning. Cellular-bonding for example is a technology which can use multiple 4G and 5G cellular signals to make one stronger reliable connection. This allows for high quality streaming to take place in more and more remote locations. Computer vision is another exciting technology powering the auto-tracking of subjects with PTZ cameras; helping to simplify camera operations for video production teams. With auto-tracking enabled PTZ cameras, a single camera operator can operate multiple PTZ cameras, including other tasks such as video switching and keeping an eye on automated multi-camera framing, eliminating the need for manually following subjects with a joystick controller.

REMOTE PRODUCTION
PRO TIP

V2 Cloud makes launching an OBS studio in the cloud easy. Follow this link to learn more.

KEY TAKEAWAYS FROM THIS CHAPTER:

1. IP-Based Technologies for Remote Production:

- IP technologies like NDI and SMPTE 2110 have revolutionized remote production by enabling high-quality video transmission over standard networks.

- NDI is accessible and ideal for smaller scale or entry-level productions due to its ease of use and low bandwidth requirements.

- SMPTE 2110 caters to high-end production needs with capabilities for uncompressed video, requiring more robust network infrastructure and technical expertise.

2. Comparative Overview of NDI and SMPTE 2110:

    - NDI offers flexibility and ease of use, making it suitable for less complex, cost-sensitive environments.

    - SMPTE 2110 provides superior video quality and precise synchronization, suited for professional broadcasting environments that demand the highest production standards.

3. Dante Video Integration:

    - Dante has extended its capabilities from audio to video, facilitating seamless interoperability across different devices and enhancing networked video production's flexibility.

4. Impact of Cloud Computing:

    - Cloud computing technologies have greatly enhanced remote production by decentralizing data processing and storage, allowing for more scalable and flexible production workflows.

    - Services like V2Cloud cater specifically to remote video production, simplifying the transition to cloud-based workflows.

5. Emerging Technologies and Trends:

    - Advancements in 5G, AI, and computer vision are pushing the boundaries of what's possible in remote production, enabling higher quality streams from remote locations and more dynamic production techniques such as auto-tracking cameras.

6. Application of Dante and Cloud Technologies:

    - Dante's expansion into video enhances system compatibility and control, while cloud services facilitate remote access and control over production, crucial for adapting to fast-changing production demands.

4 Core Principles and Genre Specific Best Practices

Video production is an art, and like any art there are core principles that every video producer and videographer should know to be successful. These core principles are the building blocks of high-quality video production, whether you're capturing a live event, creating educational content, or producing a more artistic live event experience.

This chapter will review the 180 Degree Shutter Speed Rule, ensuring your motion capture looks natural and professional. You'll learn the 180 Degree *Camera* Rule, a cornerstone of spatial continuity that keeps your audience engaged and oriented. The Rule of Thirds, a timeless compositional guideline, to help you frame your shots with balance and aesthetic appeal.

Beyond these fundamental rules, you will learn the importance of smooth camera movements, selecting the appropriate video transitions, and genre specific production tips.

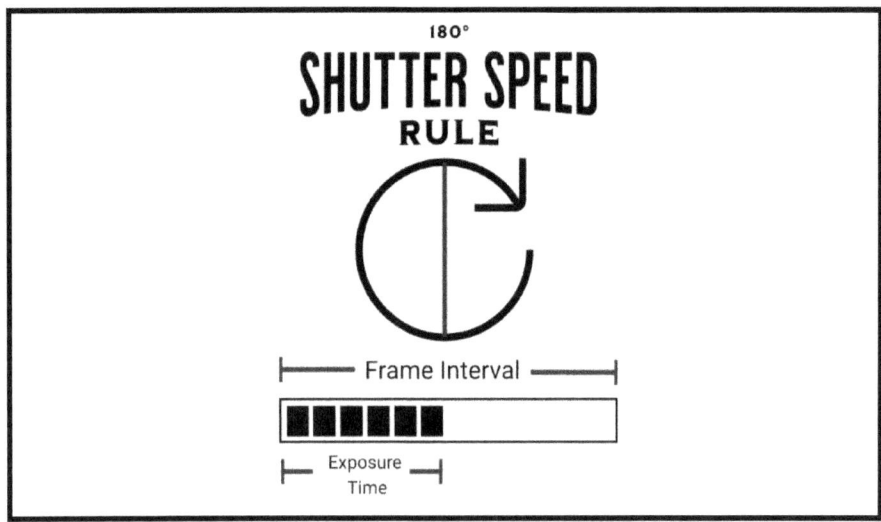

180 Degree Shutter Speed Rule

This rule ensures that your motion capture looks natural and professional by setting your shutter speed to double your frame rate.

For example, if you're shooting at 30 frames per second (fps), your shutter speed should be 1/60th of a second. This creates a natural motion blur that our eyes are accustomed to seeing.

This rule is very easy to follow, as you get into the habit of starting your productions by selecting and locking in your preferred resolution and frame rate. This practice helps to guide your shutter speed setting, which allows you to focus on adjusting the iris. The iris is the aperture of the camera lens, controlling the amount of light that enters. Proper adjustment ensures your subject remains well-exposed throughout varying lighting conditions, maintaining consistent image quality.

When the iris is fully open, more light enters the camera, resulting in a shallower depth of field and a more pronounced background blur. On the other hand, closing the iris reduces the amount of light, increasing depth of field and enhancing focus across a wider area. Understanding these effects allows for creative control over the visual style and clarity of your video productions.

You can of course break this rule to achieve interesting video effects. For example, if you reduce your shutter speed, you will see more blur in your video. If you increase your shutter speed, you will see moving objects more clearly. The 180 degree shutter speed rule is a good starting point to find a natural looking video. Remember adjusting the shutter speed also affects how much light enters the camera, so you may need to compensate by adjusting other settings such as gain, luminance or aperture. Experimenting with these variables can lead to creative outcomes, allowing you to craft videos that convey different moods and visual dynamics depending on your artistic intent and the narrative you wish to convey.

180 Degree Camera Rule (Axis of Action)

The 180 Degree Camera Rule maintains spatial continuity by keeping the camera on one side of an imaginary axis between the subjects. Crossing this line can disorient the viewer and disrupt the visual flow. Adhering to this rule ensures that your audience stays engaged and oriented.

Breaking this rule can be disorienting for viewers, especially during sporting events where viewers are tracking progress up and down a specific area. If you break this rule, it should be done intentionally knowing the non-verbal communication you will have with your audience. For example, breaking the rule could work during a half-time break or during a team huddle, when the teams are not in an active play.

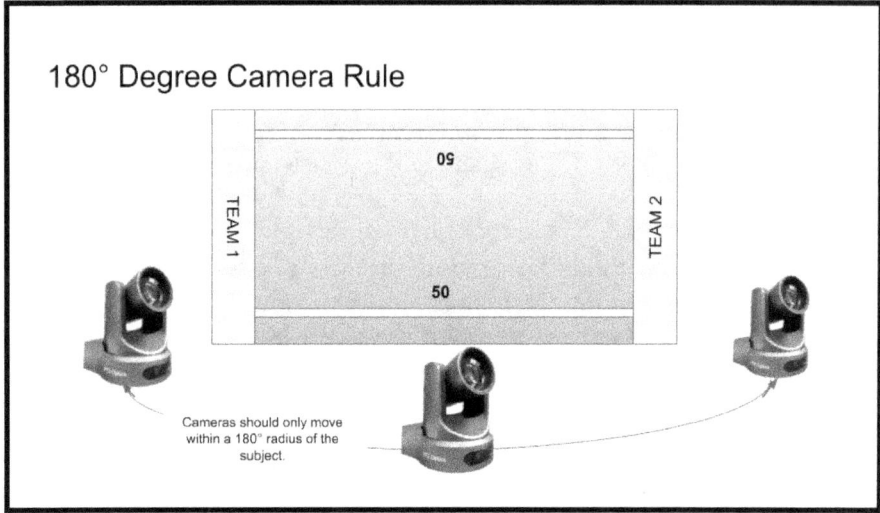

180° degree camera rule shown on a football field.

Rule of Thirds

This timeless compositional guideline divides the frame into nine equal parts using two equally spaced horizontal lines and two equally spaced vertical lines. Placing important elements along these lines or their intersections creates balanced and aesthetically pleasing shots. This simple technique can significantly enhance the visual appeal of your videos.

The rule of thirds will help to guide your shot compositions.

Framing and Composition

Good framing and composition are essential for creating visually appealing shots that draw in your audience and convey your story effectively. These elements are the foundation of visual storytelling, helping to guide the viewer's eye and emphasize the most important aspects of the scene. Here are key components to consider:

1. **Headroom**
    - Headroom refers to the space between the top of the subject's head and the top of the frame. Too much headroom can make the subject appear small and insignificant, while too little can make the composition feel cramped. A well-balanced headroom provides a comfortable view of the subject and ensures they are the focal point.
2. **Lead Room (Nose Room)**
    - Lead room is the space in front of a moving or facing subject. For example, if your subject is looking or moving to the left, provide adequate space on the left side of the frame. This technique creates a sense of direction and movement, making the composition feel natural and dynamic.
3. **Background**
    - The background can significantly impact the overall

composition of your shot. Ensure that the background complements the subject without being distracting. Pay attention to elements like lighting, color, and objects in the background, as they can add context or create visual clutter. Using shallow depth of field can help isolate the subject and blur the background for a cleaner look.

4. **Leading Lines**
    - Leading lines are visual elements that guide the viewer's eye toward the subject or through the composition. These lines can be literal, like roads or fences, or implied, like the direction of a gaze or the alignment of objects. They help create a sense of direction and focus within the frame.

5. **Framing within the Frame**
    - Using natural or artificial elements to frame your subject can add interest and focus. This technique draws attention to the subject and can add context or a sense of place. Examples include using doorways, windows, or branches to create a frame within the composition.

Smooth Camera Movements

Smooth and deliberate camera movements enhance production quality by creating a professional and polished look. Avoid unnecessary zooms and pans. If possible move your cameras before you transition to the live take. If you must move cameras while they are "live" in your production output, use tools like tripods, sliders, and gimbals to achieve fluid motion. This ensures that your audience remains focused on the content rather than distracted by camera movements.

Selecting Appropriate Video Transitions

Choosing the right video transitions can greatly impact the flow and feel of your production. Simple cuts are often the most effective, but occasionally, dissolves or wipes can add a creative touch. The key is to use transitions that complement the story and maintain the viewer's immersion.

A video transition is a non-verbal, visual signal you can use to inform your audience of the direction of your production. Therefore, you if you are consistent with the use of video transitions, you can foreshadow what the viewer should expect by using video transitions to signal specific scene transitions. After all, video transitions are a tool for transitioning between scenes. One of the most powerful uses of this is in sports productions, where fancy stingers transitions are used to transition to video that is something other than live sports. For example, the NFL will often use a fancy stringer transition to cut to instant replay footage.

1. **Cut**
    - The most common transition, used 90% of the time, is a direct switch between two video sources without any noticeable effects. Ideal for moving between live camera angles in the same scene. The cut happens in the blink of an eye, and it should be your go-to transition for most source switching.
2. **Fade**
    - Used less frequently, fades gently transition between scenes by gradually increasing or decreasing the opacity of the video, often signaling the start or end of a segment.
3. **Fade to Black**
    - A powerful transition to mark the beginning or end of a production, or to close a unique scene. It communicates nonverbally with the audience and is effective when timed with audio.
4. **Crossfade**
    - Produces a smooth, artistic effect by blending two video sources. Often used in musical performances or emotional scenes to enhance the visual experience.
5. **Stinger**
    - Stinger transitions combine visual graphics with an alpha channel layer so that the live video is mixed with graphics in a single transitional effect.

Type	Most Commonly Used
Cut	90% of the time
Fade	<5%

Other	<5%

Genre-Specific Strategies: Enhancing Your Production Quality

Different types of video productions come with unique viewer expectations. You can use the video production tools at your disposal to communicate with your audience fluidly to tell the unique story your production is designed for. Each genre of live production has its own set of audience expectations and best practices for keeping viewers engaged and informed. Let's break down some of the top live production events and the top techniques for each.

Educational

Producing live educational content requires a blend of clarity, engagement, and accessibility to create an effective learning environment. The essence of classroom interactions, detailed demonstrations, and key instructional moments can deliver a comprehensive educational experience. For viewers, particularly students, educational live productions are expected to provide clear visuals, crisp audio, and interactive elements that facilitate understanding and participation. The goal is to bridge the gap between traditional and remote learning, ensuring that educational content is engaging, informative, and accessible, ultimately enhancing the overall learning experience. For educational content, the technical decisions and choices you make should be transparent to viewers, in an effort to make the content the main focus.

1. Interactive Camera Work:

- **Dynamic Angles:** Use multiple camera angles to capture the instructor, whiteboard, and students, creating a comprehensive view of the classroom.
- **Close-Ups:** Employ close-up shots for detailed demonstrations, experiments, and important points written on the board. If you are using an auto-tracking camera, make sure the top and bottom of an instructional areas like a whiteboard are in view at all times.

2. High-Quality Audio:

- **Clear Sound:** Utilize high-quality microphones for the instructor and students to ensure clear audio, crucial for effective communication.
- **Ambient Noise Control:** Minimize background noise and use sound mixing to balance audio levels between different speakers.

3. Engaging Visual Aids:

- **On-Screen Graphics:** Incorporate graphics, slides, and annotations to highlight key points, making the content more engaging and easier to understand.
- **Document Cameras:** Use document cameras to display textbooks, diagrams, and other educational materials clearly.

4. On-Screen Text and Captions:

- **Subtitles:** Provide subtitles or captions to accommodate diverse learning needs and ensure accessibility for all students.
- **Key Points:** Display key points and summaries on-screen to reinforce learning and aid retention.

Entertainment

Producing live entertainment content is a creative endeavor that requires a blend of technical skill, artistic vision, and audience engagement. Here you can capture the vibrancy and energy of performances, whether they be concerts, theater productions, or live shows. For audiences, entertainment productions are expected to deliver a visually stunning and acoustically pleasing experience. This can be accomplished with dynamic camera work, high-quality audio, and engaging visuals. The aim is to transport viewers into the heart of the performance, making them feel as though they are part of the live audience, experiencing every thrilling moment firsthand.

1. Dynamic Camera Work:

- **Multiple Angles:** Use a variety of camera angles to capture the full scope of the performance, including wide shots, close-ups, and audience reactions.

- **Steadicam and wireless cameras:** Incorporate Steadicams and wireless cameras for smooth, cinematic movements and crowd shots that add a professional and dynamic feel.

2. High-Quality Audio:

- **Professional Microphones:** Use high-quality microphones to capture clear and balanced audio from performers, instruments, and ambient sounds.
- **Sound Mixing:** Employ sound mixing techniques to balance dialogue, music, and sound effects, ensuring a polished audio experience.

3. Engaging Visuals and Effects:

- **Lighting Design:** Utilize creative lighting to enhance the mood and highlight key moments, using spotlights, colored lights, and special effects.
- **Visual Effects:** Integrate visual effects, graphics, and animations to add excitement and visual interest to the production.

4. Seamless Transitions:

- **Smooth Cuts and Fades:** Use smooth transitions between shots to maintain the flow and energy of the performance.
- **Creative Compositions:** Experiment with creative composition techniques like split screens, picture-in-picture, and fast cuts to keep viewers engaged.

5. Audience Interaction:

- **Live Polls and Chats:** Enable live polls, chats, and social media interactions to engage the audience and make them feel part of the experience. Display these chats on screen using tools such as vMix social.
- **Real-Time Feedback:** Incorporate real-time feedback and shoutouts to acknowledge the audience and build a sense of community.

House of Worship

Producing live broadcasts for house of worship services requires a blend of technical expertise and sensitivity to the spiritual and communal aspects of the event. It involves capturing the essence of worship, including sermons, music, and congregational participation, to create a meaningful and immersive experience for remote viewers. For viewers, house of worship productions are expected to provide a seamless and respectful representation of the service, with clear audio, thoughtful camera work, and unobtrusive transitions. The aim is to foster a sense of connection and participation, allowing remote worshippers to feel spiritually engaged and part of the community, even from a distance.

1. Respectful Camera Work:

- **Discrete Movement:** Ensure camera movements are smooth and unobtrusive to maintain the reverence of the service. If you are using an auto-tracking camera, adjust the tracking sensitivity so that it is smooth and ideal for the pacing of your subject.
- **Multiple Angles:** Use multiple camera angles to capture different aspects of the service, such as the speaker, choir, congregation, and other significant areas.

2. Clear Audio Quality:

- **High-Quality Microphones:** Use high-quality microphones for the speaker, choir, and musicians to ensure clear and crisp audio.
- **Sound Mixing:** Employ sound mixing to balance the audio levels, ensuring that speech, music, and ambient sounds are appropriately blended.

3. Engaging Visuals:

- **Focus on Key Moments:** Highlight key moments like sermons, prayers, and musical performances with close-up shots and thoughtful framing.
- **Subtle Transitions:** Use gentle transitions between shots to maintain the service's serene atmosphere.

4. On-Screen Text and Graphics:

- **Lyrics and Scriptures:** Display song lyrics, scriptures, and sermon points on-screen to help remote viewers follow along and participate.
- **Announcements:** Include important announcements and messages relevant to the congregation.

5. Live Interaction:

- **Chat Moderation:** Enable live chat features where viewers can share their thoughts and prayers, with moderators to maintain a respectful environment.
- **Real-Time Feedback:** Incorporate real-time feedback options like prayer requests or questions that can be addressed during the service.

6. Lighting and Color Correction:

- **Natural Lighting:** You will often find that natural lighting changes depending on the day. Be prepared to compensate for changing lighting conditions using color correction tools.
- **Stage Lighting:** Ensure the stage is well-lit to keep the focus on the speaker and performers without being harsh or distracting.

Live Sports

Producing live sports broadcasts is a thrilling and fast-paced endeavor, requiring precision, quick decision-making, and seamless coordination among the production team. It involves capturing the high-energy action, dramatic moments, and intricate details of the game to create an engaging and immersive viewing experience. For viewers, sports live productions are expected to deliver dynamic and comprehensive coverage, complete with multiple camera angles, instant replays, real-time statistics, and expert commentary. The goal is to transport viewers to the heart of the action, providing them with an experience that is as close as possible to being at the event itself. Here are some key areas to consider:

1. Camera Placement and Angles:

- **Dynamic Coverage:** Utilize multiple camera angles to cover all

aspects of the game. Position cameras at strategic locations such as behind goals, at mid-field, and at elevated positions to capture wide shots and close-ups.
- **Tracking Shots:** Implement camera operators who can track players and the ball, ensuring that key moments are never missed. While close up shots are great, give viewers the ability to watch a play develop.

2. Instant Replay and Slow Motion:

- **Key Moments:** Use instant replays and slow-motion shots to highlight critical plays, goals, or fouls. This not only enhances viewer engagement but also provides in-depth analysis of important events.
- **Replay Systems:** Replay systems allow you to quickly cue and broadcast moments to replay and review.

3. Graphics and On-Screen Information:

- **Scoreboards and Timers:** Display real-time scores, timers, and statistics to keep viewers informed about the game's progress.
- **Player Stats:** Incorporate player statistics, team lineups, and other relevant information to add depth to the broadcast.

4. Commentary and Analysis:

- **Expert Commentary:** Cut to your commentary experts who can explain strategies, player performances, and game dynamics.
- **Halftime Analysis:** Include halftime shows with expert analysis, interviews, and highlights to keep viewers engaged during breaks.

5. Audio Quality:

- **Clear Commentary:** Ensure that commentary is clear and audible, using high-quality microphones and sound mixing.
- **Ambient Sounds:** Capture the ambient sounds of the crowd, the field, and player interactions to create an immersive experience.

By employing these techniques, you can elevate the production quality of entertainment broadcasts, creating an immersive, exciting, and memorable experience for viewers. When preparing for a live video production, understanding your tools is crucial. Tools like the StreamDeck or an xKeys can optimize your production control experience by enabling quick actions such as muting microphones, zooming cameras, calling PTZ presets, or starting recordings.

However, multitasking can be challenging for a single producer. It's often better to divide tasks among team members, including camera operations, social media management, video production, and technical setup. While some exceptional individuals can manage all these tasks, it's generally more efficient to share the workload.

Preparation is key to a successful production. This includes setting up PTZ presets for dynamic presentations and holding setup meetings to discuss workflows with your team. Despite the pressures of live production, it's important to remember to have fun and enjoy the process.

KEY TAKEAWAYS FROM THIS CHAPTER

1. Effective Task Distribution
    - Delegate responsibilities for camera operations, social media management, video production, and on-camera talent to different team members for a more efficient workflow.
2. Core Principles of Video Production
    - Understanding and mastering fundamental video production principles are essential for creating high-quality content, whether it's for live events, educational purposes, or artistic performances.
3. Selecting Appropriate Video Transitions
    - Choose video transitions that complement the story and maintain viewer immersion. Simple cuts are often effective, but creative transitions like dissolves or wipes can add a unique touch when used appropriately.

Remote Production

5 BANDWIDTH AND BITRATES

As the world of broadcasting and media continues to evolve, the shift towards remote production has started to gain momentum. You may have heard the term REMI (Remote Integration Model) in reference to "remote production" which describes the use of broadcast equipment from home or a remote location.

NDI was announced almost a decade ago in 2015 and the original promotional videos looked a lot like what we have access to today. It took a decade of software development and hardware improvements to make it dependably usable, but remote production and global video source routing is a reality. Today, everything from cameras, to encoders, audio mixers and more can be used over a network connection for remote production. Leveraging IP connectivity, broadcasters now have an array of choices to bridge their local area network (LAN) with others across the wide area network (WAN/Internet) to create remote production ecosystems that span the globe.

Bridging the Gap

Remote production not only addresses the immediate challenges faced by broadcasters, such as reducing operational costs and overcoming geographic limitations, but also opens up new markets that have been traditionally underserved. By enabling the broadcast of events from remote locations without the need for expensive on-site production setups, remote production allows live streaming professionals to cover niche sports, business & cultural events and local news in regions that previously could not justify the high costs associated with traditional broadcasting methods. This expansion into new areas not only diversifies the content available to viewers but also enhances cultural representation and inclusivity in media. Additionally, remote production provides significant business opportunities to those who are able to fulfill these services. Through these capabilities, broadcasters, corporate users and others can tap into a global market for video production services.

High-Speed Internet and Connectivity

High-speed internet enables the real-time transmission of large amounts of data, which is essential for live broadcasting. This capability allows high-quality video and audio feeds to be sent from remote locations to production studios anywhere in the world. However, while download speeds are crucial for connecting to cloud services, such as a cloud-based video mixing system or physical production hubs/control rooms it is the upload speeds that can often be the bottleneck on-location where the video and audio feeds need to be transmitted *from* the remote location. It's the same in each direction (remote-location-to-studio or cloud and studio/control room-to-remote-location); each live video and audio source that you are uploading will require bandwidth. Video production professionals will spend time configuring the bitrates for each audio and video source to get everything working properly if you have limited bandwidth.

Bandwidth is measured in bits and the word "bandwidth" is used to describe the maximum data transfer rate of your internet connection. When you measure this speed, you are measuring megabits as they relate to time. Your internet speeds are measured in upload and download speeds. Megabits-per-second (Mbps) are used to measure the size of the bandwidth "pipeline" between your computer and the internet.

Resolution	Pixel Count	Frame Rate	Quality	Bitrate
4K 60fps	3840x2160	60fps	High	60Mbps
4K 60fps	3840x2160	60fps	Medium	40Mbps
4K 60fps	3840x2160	60fps	Low	20Mbps

4K 30fps	3840x2160	30fps	High	30Mbps
4K 30fps	3840x2160	30fps	Medium	20Mbps
4K 30fps	3840x2160	30fps	Low	10Mbps
1080p60fps	1920x1080	60fps	High	12Mbps
1080p60fps	1920x1080	60fps	Medium	9Mbps
1080p60fps	1920x1080	60fps	Low	6Mbps
1080p30fps	1920x1080	30fps	High	6Mbps
1080p30fps	1920x1080	30fps	Medium	4.5Mbps
1080p30fps	1920x1080	30fps	Low	3Mbps
720p30fps	1280x720	30fps	High	3.5Mbps
720p30fps	1280x720	30fps	Medium	2.5Mbps
720p30fps	1280x720	30fps	Low	1.5Mbps

You can think about your live stream's resolution as the size of your live stream's canvas. The bitrate that you select is the amount of data that is used to fill that canvas. Therefore, you can have a high-quality 1080p stream with a bit rate of 6 Mbps, or you can have a low-quality 1080p stream with a bit rate of just 2 Mbps. Years ago, back in the time of Standard Definition video (SD) (320x240 pixels), you could use Adobe's Flash to encode and stream at roughly 500 Kbps (that's half a megabit). Today, most people will expect at a minimum of 720p video and a bit rate of at least 1~3 Mbps. New reports from Akamai show that most people watching 1080p video find that 6Mbps looks like excellent quality.

Tips for Ensuring Reliable Upload Speeds:

1. **Assess Your Needs**: Before the event, determine the bandwidth requirements for your specific media and production quality. HD and 4K streams, for example, have significantly higher upload demands and you should calculate the overall needs with 10-20% headroom for network fluctuations.

2. **Choose the Right Internet Provider**: Opt for an internet service provider that offers symmetric internet speeds; currently best using fiber-to-the-premises—where upload speeds are as high as download speeds—or one that is known for reliable upload performance.

3. **Dedicated Connections**: Consider using a dedicated line or "managed/dedicated bandwidth" from the IT department at your remote location to avoid sharing bandwidth with other users, which can affect upload & download speeds. In most cases, you should stay away from WiFi unless absolutely necessary.

4. **Backup Solutions**: Always have a backup internet solution ready, such as a cellular bonding router (with multiple cellular modems), a mobile hotspot, or satellite internet, to ensure continuity in case of primary connection failure. Automatic fail-over planning is essential and can include bonding cellular, ethernet and even wifi together.

5. **Test Thoroughly**: Conduct multiple dry runs at different times of the day to test the stability and reliability of your upload speeds, adjusting as necessary to optimize for actual event conditions.

By paying close attention to these factors, broadcasters can mitigate potential issues with upload speeds and ensure that their remote production operations run smoothly and efficiently.

KEY TAKEAWAYS FROM THIS CHAPTER:

1. Global Connectivity and IP Networks:
    - Remote production leverages IP connectivity, allowing broadcasters to create interconnected ecosystems that span globally. This connectivity bridges local area networks with wide area networks, facilitating the global routing of video sources.

2. Importance of High-Speed Internet and Connectivity:

    - High-speed internet is crucial for the real-time transmission of high-quality video and audio feeds essential for live broadcasting. Both upload and download speeds are vital, with a particular emphasis on upload speeds at remote locations.

3. Bandwidth Considerations and Management:

    - Effective bandwidth management is critical for remote production. Broadcasters must configure bitrates carefully based on available bandwidth to ensure quality streaming, considering both resolution and stream quality.

4. Optimization for Remote Production:

    - Regular testing and optimization of upload speeds, choosing the right internet service provider, and planning for network fluctuations are essential steps to ensure the efficiency and reliability of remote production setups.

6 CORE COMPONENTS OF REMOTE PRODUCTION

In the rapidly evolving world of broadcast, the transition to remote production is made possible by several core components. Similar to how video meetings have replaced many in-person meetings, remote production is replacing many on-site productions when appropriate. While remote production isn't just another "zoom meeting", the technology for remote camera control, video switching and editing has come a long way. In this chapter we will review the essential components of remote production and the roles they play in broadcasting projects.

Nate Hall of Stream Virtual Production packs up for "Just another Zoom call."

The Role of Technology in Remote Production

- **Audio**: Audio mixers, microphones and the required cabling are crucial for ensuring clear and synchronized sound, which is as important as video quality in maintaining professional broadcast standards.

- **Video Contribution and Encoding**: Essential for capturing high-definition video feeds and compressing them for efficient transmission back to the central production hub.

-**Cameras & Mounting Equipment**: Cameras may include a built-in encoder or need to be connected to an external encoder. ounting solutions are used to provide the necessary stability and positioning for the best camera angles. Options range from traditional tripods, which offer portability and ease of setup, to more permanent fixtures like wall or ceiling mounts that are ideal for fixed studio environments.

- **Robotic Cameras**: Provide remotely controllable camera functions such as pan, tilt and zoom. Robotic pan, tilt and zoom (PTZ) cameras are designed for remote operation and feature functionality for camera adjustments such as iris, shutter speed, and white balance.

- **Control Systems and Software**: Enable remote direction of robotic camera operations, switching, and overall production management, ensuring that producers can make real-time decisions as if they were onsite.

- **Graphics and Visual Elements**: Provide the visual enhancements that audiences expect from professional broadcasts, including lower-thirds, scoreboards, and other real-time graphics.

- **Central Production Hub/Control Room**: This can be anywhere in the world and staffed by a "one-man-band" (director/technical director) or include multiple production pros. Remote participants can be brought into the program via Zoom, Teams, Vmix, LiveU or other tools and combined with graphics, PowerPoint, playback videos, interactive polls and much more. Audio engineers, Zoom "pinners" and presenter "wranglers" often round out the crew. Equipment includes a production switcher like Blackmagic ATEM, Grass Valley Karrera, Ross Carbonite, Tricaster, Vmix or OBS, a number of laptops or mini PCs or dedicated software like Zoom ISO or LiveToAir.

White Label Webcasting's Control Center.

The Control Center includes a Zoom pinning area for a second operator (with 9 Nuc PCs), 8 iso recorders, an 80x80 routing switcher, LiveU server, back-up production PC, standby power generator and dual WAN router (with automatic failover from Fios to Comcast).

- **Communications (Comms):** Clear, low-latency communications among team members is essential to successful remote production. Back-up systems are often-overlooked but are equally critical components too. Unity Intercom is one of the most popular cloud-based or in-studio, server-based solutions available. With its flexible cost model, multiple channels for groups, one-to-one private lines, very high-quality audio and program audio integration, Unity Intercom is used worldwide by large professional broadcasters and small teams alike. And to back-up a system like this, audio conference bridges like the always-on Turbobridge are a good choice. The conference automatically begins when the second person calls in and participants do not need any kind of pin or passcode to join. Though this is a single-channel back-up solution (and you could always employ multiple bridges), it's a very fast, very reliable and inexpensive "insurance policy."

- **Networking Equipment**: Networking equipment is essential for IP-video and increasingly valuable for powering power over ethernet (PoE) enabled devices. Consideration should be made for the potential use of virtual private networks (VPNs), virtual local area networks (VLANs) — to keep your network segment separated from others — and dedicated private links are all integral for maintaining security. Network performance monitoring & management tools play an important role in optimizing network performance, enabling technicians to make real-time adjustments to ensure continuous, high-quality streams.

-**Internet Connectivity**: Reliable internet connectivity is the backbone of remote production. Cellular bonding, the ability to combine multiple cellular network connections, can enhance connection reliability and bandwidth in areas with limited connectivity options. Planning for and testing internet connectivity involves understanding the specifics of the event location and may require arrangements with local internet service providers or the deployment of mobile internet units to ensure robust and uninterrupted internet service

Audio Tools and Management

Audio quality is a fundamental aspect of broadcasting, with its importance on par with that of video quality for ensuring a professional production outcome. Effective management of audio tools ensures that sound captured at remote locations is not only clear but also well-synchronized and seamlessly integrated into the final broadcast. Here, we delve deeper into the key technologies, techniques, and practices essential for optimizing audio in remote productions.

1. **High-Quality Microphones:**
   - **Lapel/Lavalier Mics**: Ideal for interviews and talk shows, these small microphones can be discreetly clipped to clothing, offering excellent voice capture while minimizing ambient noise.
   - **Shotgun Mics**: Best for capturing audio in larger spaces or from a distance, these microphones have a directional pick-up pattern that focuses on the sound directly in front, reducing side and background noise.
   - **Condenser Mics**: Often used in studio settings, these powered mics are highly sensitive and ideal for capturing detailed soundscapes and higher frequencies.

2. **Digital Audio Mixers**:
   - These mixers allow precise control over audio levels, inputs, and outputs, and often include advanced features like auto-mixing, multiple types of equalization, dynamics processing, and effects, which help tailor the audio to the desired output quality.

3. **USB Audio Interfaces**:
   - An essential tool for converting microphone signals into digital format for computers and streaming devices. High-quality interfaces ensure minimal latency and high fidelity in sound reproduction.

4. **Advanced Audio Solutions**:

   - **Digital Audio Workstations (DAWs)**: Software such as ProTools or Audacity can be used for more complex multi-track recording, editing and mixing of audio tracks post-capture.

- **Audio over Internet Protocol (AoIP) Solutions**: Technologies like Dante or AES67 allow for the high-quality transmission of audio over IP networks, facilitating seamless remote audio integration.
   - **Cloud-Based Audio Collaboration Services:** Some TV production facilities use remote audio studios so they can focus on the video. Online services like Cloudmovers provide a variety of very high quality tools at reasonable prices.

5. **Noise-Cancellation Software:**
   - Software solutions that use algorithms to filter out background noise, ensuring that the primary audio source is clear and free of interruptions or distractions. One of our favorites is a VST3 plug-in called NS1 by Waves. Many software video production solutions such as vMix support VST3 plug-ins to enhance audio quality with the inputs you have in your system.

You can learn about Advanced IP Audio Tools for Remote Production in Chapter 10, Advanced Topics in Remote Production.

Audio-Video Encoders

Encoders combining audio and video streams are essential in remote productions for compressing and converting audiovisual data into a suitable format for streaming. These devices ensure that audio is synchronized with video during encoding, thus maintaining lip-sync and timing across the production workflow. Encoders often support various audio formats and provide adjustments for audio delay, helping to align audio precisely with the corresponding video feed. You will generally find encoders that accept audio embedded via HDMI or SDI along with encoders that feature dedicated XLR and 3.5mm audio inputs.

Best Practices for Managing Audio in Remote Productions:

1. **Soundchecks and Monitoring:**

- Conduct thorough soundchecks before going live to ensure all audio sources are correctly set up and functioning. Continuous monitoring during the broadcast is crucial to catch and adjust any issues in real time.

2. **Synchronization Techniques:**
   - Employ timecode synchronization or use clapperboards at remote sites to align audio with video in post-production. This is essential to avoid sync issues that can distract the audience. Software-based production switchers like Vmix also allow you to delay audio to match video. Viewing recorded footage of a clapboard or hand clap can guide you in how much delay to use (in milliseconds). One video frame (at 30 frames/second) equals 33.33 milliseconds).

3. **Acoustic Treatment:**
   - When setting up remote broadcasts, consider the acoustics of the environment. Utilizing pop filters, windshields, and even temporary baffling can significantly improve audio quality by reducing echo and background noise.

4. **Feedback Suppression:** One simple method to minimize feedback from public address (PA) systems is proper speaker placement that accounts for where open mics will be used. Another is to "ring out the room" which creates feedback (in multiple frequencies) and then uses graphic or parametric equalization (EQ) to lower the offending frequencies. Using both methods together is recommended. Also, auto mic-mixing functions in digital mixers typically use a gain-sharing methodology to automatically lower the volume of mics not currently in use and maintain consistent gain before feedback; significantly reducing its likelihood.

5. **Remote Audio Feeds Management:**
   - Use mix-minus setups to feed the audio back to remote contributors without including their own audio, preventis confusing echoes and delays.

6. **Redundancy:**
 - Always have backup audio sources and transmission paths. This could mean additional microphones, recording devices, or even parallel audio transmission routes to ensure that the broadcast can continue smoothly in case of technical difficulties.

Implementing these technologies and adhering to these practices ensures that audio quality in remote productions meets professional standards, providing a clear and engaging auditory experience to accompany the visual elements of the broadcast. This holistic approach to audio management not only enhances the quality of the production but also enriches the viewer's experience, making the content more impactful and enjoyable.

Remote Audio Production

Remote audio production software enables audio professionals to work seamlessly from almost anywhere. This shift is supported by various innovative remote audio recording and collaboration software solutions, each tailored to meet the diverse needs of the music and broadcasting industries. Audio mixers with remote production control applications will be covered in our hardware chapter later in this book.

You can learn more about remote audio production in Chapter 10, Advanced Topics in Remote Production.

Video Contribution and Encoding

In remote production, a common saying is "the last mile is the longest mile." This phrase emphasizes the challenges of delivering the live broadcast signal from a remote location to the central studio. It highlights issues like latency, bandwidth limitations, and signal integrity that are critical for maintaining high quality and reliability in the broadcast. This saying conveys that despite being a short distance, the "last mile" involves significant technological and logistical challenges, making it the most crucial part of the production process. In some cases, remote productions still use traditional SDI and HDMI video sources which are then encoded and streamed to the far end. In other cases, cameras and audio devices are IP-native featuring built-in NDI, Dante, AES67 or SMPTE 2110 outputs.

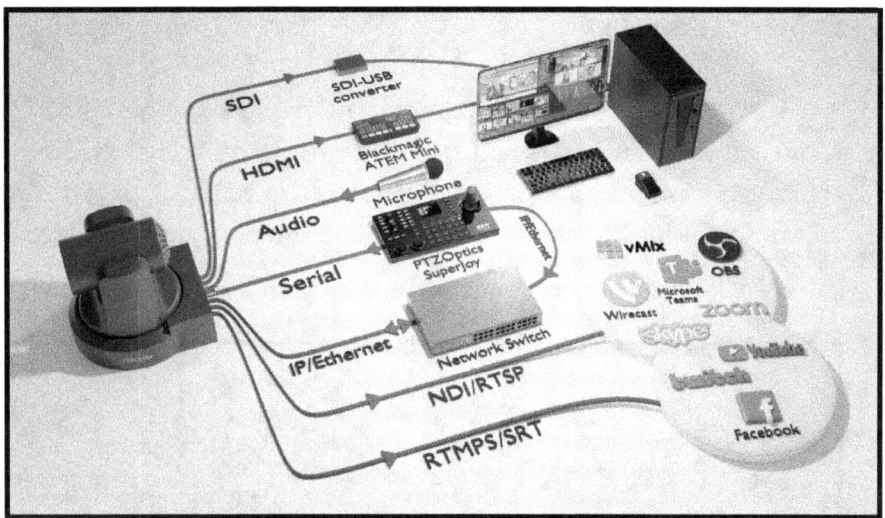

PTZOptics camera connection diagram.

The diagram above outlines the use of every port on the back of an IP-connected PTZOptics Move SE camera. The SDI connection is ideal for long cable runs, and it is connected to an SDI to USB capture card (dongle/converter) which is connected to a computer used for encoding and streaming the video. The HDMI connection is shown connected to a Blackmagic ATEM Mini, a popular video mixer used to mix multiple HDMI video sources into a single USB connection to the computer. The 3.5mm audio connection is shown with a microphone used to embed audio into the HDMI, SDI, NDI and other IP video streams. It's important to note that most PTZ cameras will only accept a line level audio input, so some microphones will require a mixer or a pre-amp audio interface to boost the signal. A serial connection is shown for use with a local PTZ joystick controller, although network connections are generally preferred for remote production. NDI and

RTSP video is shown for use with software solutions such as vMix, Wirecast, OBS and Zoom. Finally, RTMPS and SRT are shown for live streaming video to CDNs such as Facebook and YouTube. SRT video can also be used to send video to live production software on the LAN or in the cloud. vMix can accept SRT directly from cameras and other encoders which is particularly useful in virtual environments.

Capture Technologies

The first step in the video contribution process involves capturing your audio and video sources. The next step is often getting those video sources to a remote location using your internet connection. When you are working with IP-native video and audio sources, you can reduce the need for many hardware capture devices.

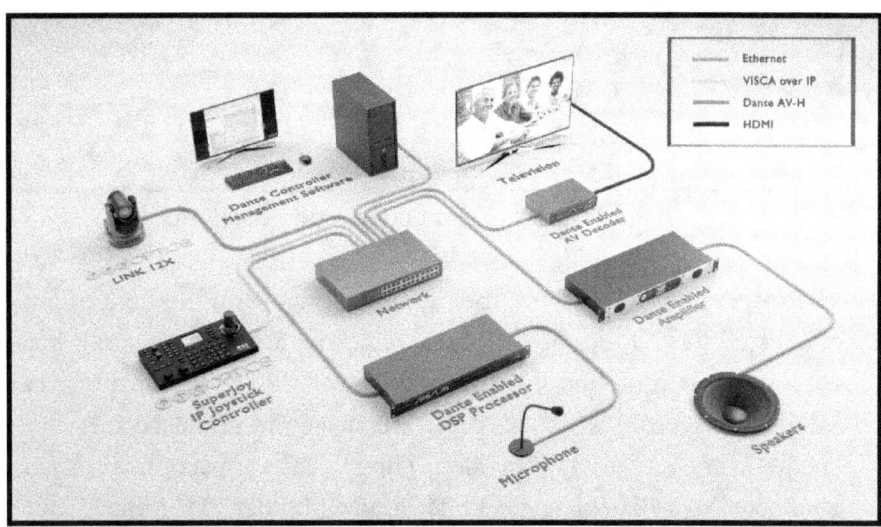

Dante AV-H workflow including a camera, a DSP, a decoder and an amplifier.

The diagram above shows a Dante AV-H workflow in a meeting room environment. The PTZOptics Link 4K is a Dante AV-H enabled camera which can be managed by the Dante ecosystem of software tools. The Link 4K is used to send video to a video meeting client using Dante Studio's virtual webcam output. The Dante Controller software can then be used to manage both the camera, the DSP and the Dante-enabled amplifier in the room. All of the intelligent devices are network connected, leaving only specific devices such as the speakers and microphones as analog connection points.

Many cameras now include built-in encoding for streaming audio and video on the LAN via NDI, RTSP or Dante AV-H. It's not uncommon for cameras to stream over the WAN reliably via transport protocols such as SRT or RTMP(S). Today many cameras support embedded NDI and Dante audio/video connectivity which allows for remote production using NDI Bridge and Dante Connect.

PTZOptics Hive-linked cameras, for example, allow for remote connections to the Hive remote production software. These cameras can be set up once to link with your unique Hive Studio and then shipped to a remote location for instant connectivity once they are connected to the internet. Dedicated remote production devices like these are called "edge devices" as they sit on the edge of the LAN and are designed to connect to the cloud easily without additional configuration.

Capture cards are hardware devices that convert video signals into a digital format that can be easily transmitted or stored. Popular capture cards include simple HDMI to USB adapters and more advanced HDMI and SDI PCIe capture cards. They play a critical role in capturing uncompressed video and bringing them into a production computer for encoding.

Screen Capture

Capturing the video content from a computer screen is often done with software. Screen sharing is often used in video communications solutions such as Microsoft Teams and Zoom. Video communications software can be used as a screen capture tool, but oftentimes broadcasters are looking for a high quality video capture along with remote control over the screen they are capturing.

NDI Screen Capture is a tool that is available to capture the screen of any computer that it has access to. NDI Screen Capture HX is a new "High Efficiency" version of the tool, which can capture video from any screen on the computer the software is installed on. The tool can then output that video via NDI on the LAN. NDI Screen Capture has the capability to capture video from a screen and any webcam also attached to the computer. This is ideal for scenarios such as eSports where broadcasters want to capture the on-screen gameplay along with a webcam of the player.

Many times, remote production experts use software such as vMix to capture a screen and send it over the internet using vMix Call. vMix Call is a technology used both to link two vMix systems together and to bring-in remote participants for live interviews. The number of vMix Call inputs you can create is limited by your vMix plan. One of the nice features of vMix Call is the simple link sharing option to get remote guests into a vMix production. The system is very easy to use and it handles all the complex mix-minus audio for remote guests which eliminates echoes that can be introduced with sending audio back and forth between remote sides of a call.

Another useful tool in the world of remote production is Internet Clicker; a tool that allows remote presenters themselves to click through their slides that you may be hosting for them. The tool is incredibly simple and is often used by presenters who are not next to their laptop, but it also works for those who are remote to the computer location. Internet Clicker allows you to send simple messages to your remote presenters and give them the peace of mind that you are there as a remote producer backing-them-up to push their slides along during their presentations if they don't, can't or lose control.

Video Encoding

Once video is captured during a production, it can be encoded and sent around the world. Encoding is the critical process of compressing video files so that they can be easily transmitted over networks without consuming excessive bandwidth. H.264, H.265, and VP9 are the three prominent video codecs, each offering distinct advantages and drawbacks. H.264, widely known for its broad compatibility across devices and platforms, strikes a balance between video quality and compression, making it ideal for general streaming and broadcasting.

H.265, or High Efficiency Video Codec (HEVC), enhances compression efficiency significantly, reducing bandwidth up to 50% compared to H.264 while maintaining the same quality. This makes it well-suited for high-resolution video such as 4K and 8K. However, H.265 is not as universally supported and requires more processing power, which could be a hindrance for devices with limited capabilities.

VP9, developed by Google, offers similar compression benefits as H.265 but without any associated royalty fees, making it a cost-effective alternative. It's particularly effective for platforms like YouTube that prioritize reduced bandwidth usage. However, VP9's drawback is its limited hardware support and high computational demand for encoding and decoding.

The AV1 encoding codec is another significant advancement in video compression technology. Developed by the Alliance for Open Media, AV1 aims to provide high-quality video streams while reducing data usage significantly compared to its predecessors, such as VP9 and H.264. As an open-source and royalty-free codec, AV1 is designed to be used widely across the internet, especially for streaming video content at reduced bandwidths without compromising on video quality. Major tech companies like Google, Microsoft, Amazon, and Netflix support AV1 due to its efficiency and potential to improve streaming experiences in an era of increasing demand for high-definition and ultra-high-definition video content.

Codec	Compression Efficiency	Quality at Low Bitrates	Latency	Compatibility	Royalty-Free
H.264 (AVC)	Good	Good	Low	Very High (Ubiquitous)	No
H.265 (HEVC)	Better	Better	Medium	High (Widespread)	No
VP9	Better	Better	High	Moderate (Limited by device and platform support)	Yes
AV1	Best	Best	High	Growing (Supported on newer devices and platforms)	Yes

This comparison table outlines the key attributes of popular video codecs—H.264, H.265, VP9, and AV1—highlighting their differences in compression efficiency, performance at low bitrates, latency, compatibility across devices, and licensing costs to aid in selecting the most suitable codec for specific video production and streaming needs.

Selecting the right codec and encoding settings is crucial for optimizing both the quality and the efficiency of video broadcasts. This choice significantly depends on balancing quality with bandwidth constraints and the specific needs of the content being delivered.

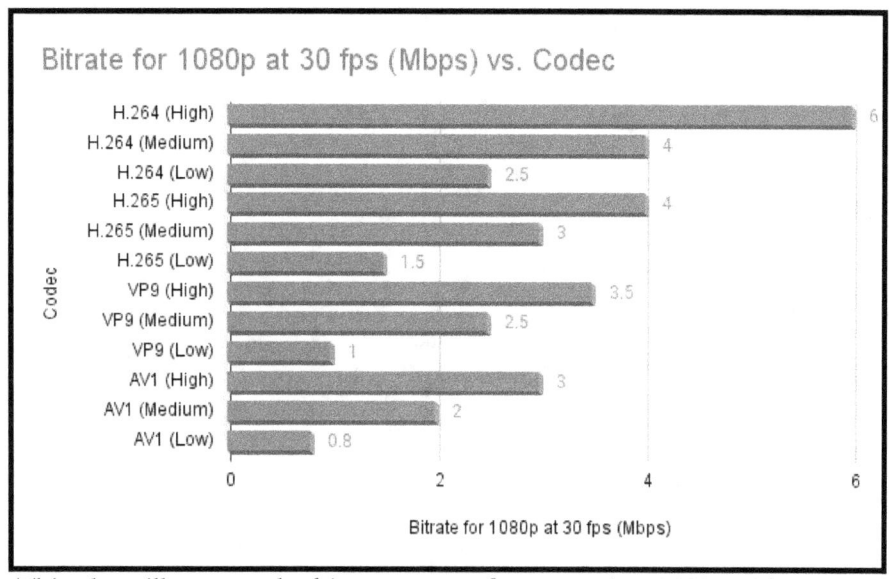

This chart illustrates the bitrate ranges for streaming 1080p video at 30 fps using H.264, H.265, VP9, and AV1.

Quality	Codec	Bitrate for 1080p at 30 fps (Mbps)
High	H.264	4.0 - 6.0 Mbps
Medium	H.264	2.5 - 4.0 Mbps
Low	H.264	1.0 - 2.5 Mbps
High	H.265	2.5 - 4.0 Mbps
Medium	H.265	1.5 - 3.0 Mbps

Low	H.265	0.7 - 1.5 Mbps
High	VP9	2.0 - 3.5 Mbps
Medium	VP9	1.0 - 2.5 Mbps
Low	VP9	0.5 - 1.0 Mbps
High	AV1	1.5 - 3.0 Mbps
Medium	AV1	0.8 - 2.0 Mbps
Low	AV1	0.3 - 0.8 Mbps

For live broadcasts, where real-time encoding is necessary, using efficient hardware or software encoders that can quickly process and compress video feeds is essential. These encoders must be capable of handling high-quality streams while minimizing latency, ensuring the broadcast remains as close to real-time as possible. Low-latency is particularly critical in live events such as sports, concerts or interactive corporate events where even a slight delay can disrupt the viewer experience.

When configuring your encoder, one common setting to consider is whether to use Variable Bit Rate (VBR) or Constant Bit Rate (CBR). VBR allows the bitrate to fluctuate depending on the complexity of the video frame. This can be beneficial in scenarios where video quality is prioritized over bandwidth consistency. For example, in a live concert broadcast, using VBR might be appropriate as it can allocate more bits to more complex scenes, ensuring high-quality video during fast-moving performances while reducing the bitrate during slower, simpler segments.

Conversely, CBR maintains a consistent bitrate throughout the broadcast, which is ideal for environments with strict bandwidth limitations, such as streaming sports events over constrained network conditions. CBR ensures a predictable rate of data flow, which can simplify network planning and management, reducing the likelihood of buffering and ensuring a smooth viewer experience.

In addition to bitrate settings, reducing your stream's bitrate outright might be necessary when dealing with very limited bandwidth or when broadcasting to viewers with lower-quality internet connections. For instance, during a live webinar where the visual content might not be as dynamic (such as simple slide presentations or talking heads), lowering the bitrate can still deliver a clear enough image while conserving bandwidth and improving accessibility for participants with slower connections.

Employing these efficient encoding techniques and tools is vital for achieving low-latency transmissions, which are essential for maintaining the immediacy and fluidity of live broadcasts. Carefully choosing between VBR and CBR, as well as adjusting the bitrate according to the content type and network conditions, will significantly impact the success and quality of the broadcast.

Contribution Links

There are so many great ways to get video into your remote production system. These days, a modern smartphone running several app choices from Larix Broadcaster to Zoom can upload strong 1080p video signals over a WiFi connection. The latest advancements in WiFi technology, specifically WiFi 6 and the emerging WiFi 6E, have significantly improved the capabilities of wireless networks to handle such data-intensive tasks. WiFi 6, also known as 802.11ax, increases the network efficiency and speed, supports a greater number of connected devices, and reduces latency compared to its predecessors. This is particularly beneficial for uploading high-definition video, as WiFi 6 can effectively manage the increased data throughput and maintain a stable connection even in crowded environments.

Furthermore, WiFi 6E extends these capabilities by adding additional spectrum in the 6 GHz band, which means more bandwidth and less interference for connected devices. This is crucial when transmitting high-resolution video content from smartphones, as it requires substantial bandwidth. For instance, uploading a 1080p video at a good quality might need between 3 to 6 Mbps of upload speed, while 4K video can demand upwards of 25 Mbps. With WiFi 6's enhanced data handling capabilities, you should experience fewer disruptions and better video quality during live streams or remote video uploads, making it ideal for high-demand applications in remote production environments. This ensures that content creators can rely on their home or studio WiFi to deliver professional-grade video output, leveraging their smartphones as powerful broadcasting tools.

The most popular tried and true way to send audio and video is, of course, a dedicated network using Ethernet cabling. The great thing about Ethernet is that it can generally be used to power your devices by using a PoE (Power over Ethernet) network switch. When you are choosing a network switch, you should consider the specific requirements of your network, such as speed, number of ports, and PoE capabilities.

Ethernet Cabling

When setting up a network for audio and video transmission, the choice of Ethernet cabling is crucial. There are several types of Ethernet cables, including:

- **Cat 5e**: This is the standard Ethernet cable and supports speeds up to 1 Gbps up to 100 meters. It's suitable for most applications but might not be adequate for the highest quality video over large distances.
- **Cat 6**: Capable of speeds up to 10 Gbps up to 55 meters, Cat 6 is more suitable for environments requiring higher bandwidth, such as 4K video streaming.
- **Cat 6a**: Extends Cat 6 capabilities to 100 meters with speeds up to 10 Gbps, making it ideal for professional audio and video networks.
- **Cat 7**: Offers speeds up to 10 Gbps up to 100 meters but includes additional shielding to reduce signal interference, beneficial in high-interference environments like studios with multiple electronic devices.

Network Switches

Network switches are central to managing traffic in a network. They can be broadly categorized into:

- **Unmanaged Switches**: These provide basic connectivity without any configuration needed, suitable for small setups or where simplicity is prioritized.
- **Managed Switches**: Offer advanced features such as VLANs, network management, and troubleshooting tools. These are essential for larger networks or when precise control over the network traffic is needed.
- **PoE Switches**: Power over Ethernet switches can power devices through the Ethernet cable, eliminating the need for separate power supplies for devices like cameras and microphones. This is highly beneficial in AV setups to reduce cable clutter.

Setting Up a Dedicated Network for NDI or Dante

When setting up a dedicated network for NDI (network device interface) or Dante (digital audio network through ethernet), both of which are standards used for transmitting video and audio signals over Ethernet, consider the following:

- **Bandwidth Requirements**: Both NDI and Dante can be bandwidth-intensive, especially at higher resolutions and audio channel counts. Ensure your network infrastructure supports the required data rates.
- **Quality of Service (QoS)**: It's crucial to manage network traffic prioritization to ensure that audio and video data packets receive priority over less sensitive data.
- **Redundancy**: Implementing redundancy in network design, such as dual network interfaces and switches, can prevent downtime and ensure continuous availability.
- **Security**: As these networks often carry sensitive or proprietary content, implementing network security measures, including VLANs and firewalls, is crucial.

With the right combination of Ethernet cabling and network switches, a well-configured network can robustly handle the demands of NDI or Dante, providing high-quality audio and video transmission with minimal latency and interference.

Practical Applications

Sports broadcasting often involves multiple camera setups designed to capture diverse angles, making robust encoding systems necessary to handle fast-moving images and multiple feeds simultaneously. The dynamic nature of sports events, with rapid changes and high-speed action, demands high-efficiency codecs and powerful encoding hardware to ensure smooth and clear transmission.

Live concerts present unique challenges for remote production, typically employing a combination of fixed and mobile cameras to capture the dynamic nature of the performances. These events require audio synchronization and real-time encoding, as the essence of live music relies heavily on audio-visual alignment and quality. Ensuring that the visuals match the live audio output without delay is crucial for maintaining the immersive experience of live concerts. Image magnification or (IMAG) is common in these scenarios where live video is shown on large displays and must be in-sync with the real-time performance. To address the fact that digital switching software and other hardware and software components can each add some latency, care must be taken when creating digital video signal paths for IMAG to create as little latency as possible—often using a zero-latency splitter, distribution amplifier or routing switcher, such as Blackmagic Design's 80x80 routing switcher.

Control Systems and Software

Effective control over the various elements of a remote production is crucial for ensuring a seamless broadcast. This section explores the control systems and software that enable directors and producers to manage and orchestrate live broadcasts from centralized locations, handling everything from camera movements to real-time editing.

Remote Control Software

Remote control software forms the central nervous system of remote production, allowing production teams to manage equipment and broadcasts from afar:

- **Camera Control**: Software solutions enable remote operators to control camera settings such as zoom, focus, and pan, mimicking the actions of a camera operator on-site. PTZOptics Hive is the best example of this. NDI-bridge is also an interesting application when paired with NDI compatible PTZ joystick controllers.

- **Video Switching**: Directors can switch between different video feeds, choosing which camera angle goes live at any moment, all through remote interfaces. Cloud-based video switching solutions such as LiveU Studio switch between RTMP and SRT video feeds in the cloud. Other solutions such as an OBS or vMix cloud deployment are discussed later in chapter 6.

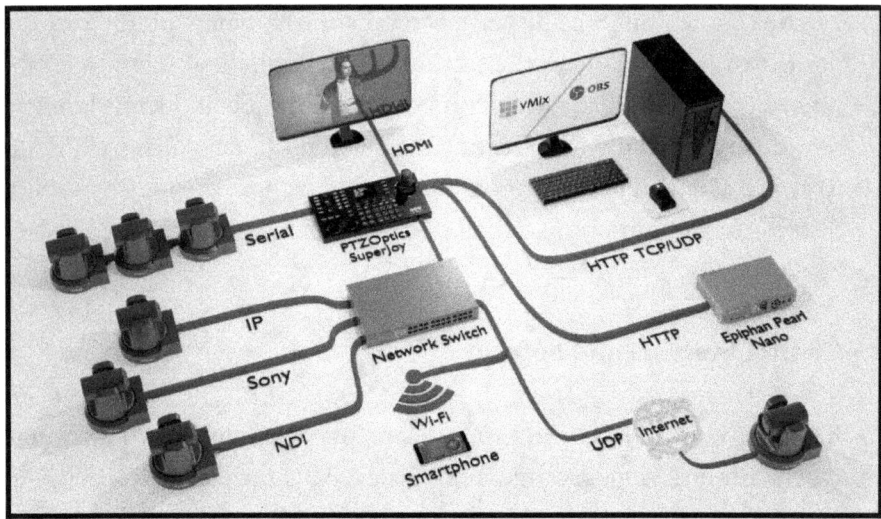

The image above shows the SuperJoy connected to several cameras on the LAN and one camera over the WAN using UDP.

Graphics and Visual Elements

Graphics and visual elements are important components of modern broadcasting, significantly enhancing the viewer's experience by adding context, information, and aesthetic appeal. In remote production environments, the integration of these elements must be managed efficiently and seamlessly to maintain high broadcast quality. There are several HTML (web browser-based) graphics solutions that have become increasingly more popular for remote production because of their simple web-based integration options. Many video switching systems, both via software and in the cloud, support HTML graphics overlays.

Graphics engines can be as simple as providing a lower third or as complex as 3D virtual sets and overlays. The adoption of cloud-based graphics solutions has improved how graphics are handled in remote productions. One great way to manage graphics for remote productions is through a cloud-based datasource. For example, you set up your lower-thirds system in vMix to pull in titles from a Google sheet. In this way, anyone on the team can update a Google Sheet entry, to dynamically change the name in a lower third title.

Singular.live is a popular web-native graphics platform that eliminates the need for dedicated, virtualized hardware by using elastic computing. This approach ensures the system is always ready and scalable. Users can access, share, collaborate, and operate Singular from anywhere in the world, making it an ideal solution for remote production environments.

Singular.live can be brought into most video production software via a simple HTML overlay. It has tools for building custom graphics from scratch or modifying templates, without the need for dongles or additional hardware, facilitating real-time collaboration and ease of use. Additionally, Singular.live is designed for remote operation, enabling users to control live graphics via proprietary apps or develop custom interfaces using the platform's SDK and API for a more tailored experience.

Singular.live also supports data streams for real-time, low-latency data, and even Google Sheets, enhancing the dynamic insertion of live data into broadcasts. Singular.live provides comprehensive educational support through its portal, where users can enhance their skills in HTML and JavaScript, ensuring they fully leverage the platform's capabilities. These features make Singular.live an invaluable tool for modern, dynamic media production environments, providing the flexibility and tools necessary for efficient and innovative live graphic management.

Graphics and visual elements are utilized extensively across various types of remote productions. In sports broadcasting, real-time updating of scores, player stats, game clocks, instant replays, and highlight indicators are all managed through sophisticated graphics systems. For news and live events, lower-thirds, informational panels, and interactive graphics, such as polling data, are integrated seamlessly to enhance narrative delivery and provide essential information to the audience.

Conclusion

Successful remote production depends not only on the performance of each individual component but also on their seamless integration into a cohesive system. With a clear grasp of these fundamental elements, broadcasters are better equipped to deliver compelling, high-quality content that meets the demands of today's diverse and dispersed audiences.

KEY TAKEAWAYS FROM THIS CHAPTER:
1. Core Components:
    a. **Audio**: Essential tools include audio mixers, microphones, and cabling to ensure clear, synchronized sound. Audio over IP can make management of audio sources easier and more efficient especially for remote production.
    b. **Video**: Video capture and encoding systems are critical for sending video feeds for remote production.
    c. **Control System**s: Software that allows for remote control of cameras and other equipment, helps to facilitate remote production.
    d. **Graphics**: Visual enhancements such as lower-thirds and scoreboards should meet professional broadcast expectations.
    e. **Switching and Delivery**: The software and hardware that control what the audiences see, including live switching and encoding are at the core of any control hub.

f. **Robotic Cameras**: PTZ cameras support remote operation with features for pan, tilt, and zoom and include audio inputs to insure synchronization between audio and video.
g. **Networking Equipment**: Selecting the right equipment for your needs is crucial for handling IP-video and powering devices.
h. **Internet Connectivity:** Fundamental for remote production. Professionals use a variety of connection types including WiFi, hard-wired internet, and cellular bonding to enhance reliability in less connected areas.

7 IP Video Production Fundamentals

IP Video, which stands for Internet Protocol Video, has changed the way video is distributed over networks, making it a cornerstone of modern remote production. Utilizing IP networks for video distribution means employing a set of standards designed for communicating over computer networks. Devices in the IP video ecosystem include cameras, switchers (both hardware and software), graphic workstations, and displays. Among the various types of IP Video, NDI® has emerged as a popular standard, especially useful in live streaming and remote video production due to its efficiency and scalability.

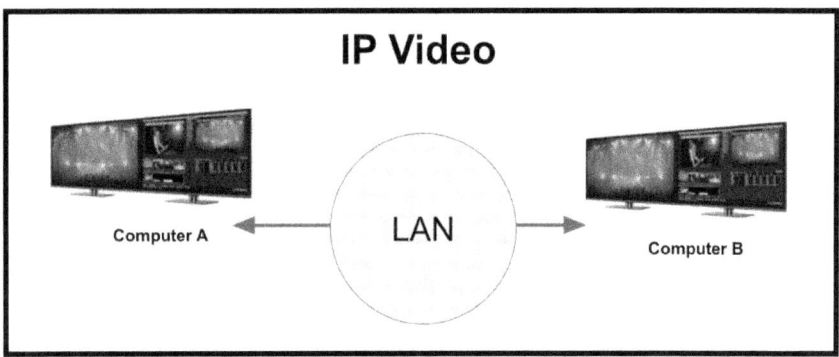

An IP video connection between two computers.

Advantages of IP Video for Remote Production

Scalability and Flexibility:
IP video significantly simplifies the scaling process in remote production environments. Unlike traditional setups that rely on HDMI or SDI cabling, which can quickly become complex and limited by hardware constraints, IP video allows for a more dynamic addition of sources. A single Ethernet cable can manage multiple video sources without the need for additional hardware switchers or capture cards, reducing both cost and complexity.

Decentralized Distribution:
Traditional video production often requires all sources to be routed to a central location—typically a hardware switcher. IP video eliminates this necessity by enabling sources to be accessed and distributed anywhere within the network. IP video is also generally bidirectional meaning more than just video can flow back and forth between devices. For example, NDI can send tally light status, PTZ controls, metadata and even KVM (Kernel-based Virtual Machine) controls to remotely control a computer with your keyboard and mouse.

Overcoming Distance Limitations:
While traditional cabling like SDI offers longer reach than HDMI, it still has physical and quality-dependent limitations. Ethernet cabling used in IP video setups not only extends reach but also supports video transmission, device control, and even power over a single connection. This capability is essential for remote productions that may span large areas or multiple locations.

Cost-Effectiveness:
IP video reduces the financial barrier to entry for high-quality video production. Traditional setups require expensive hardware such as capture cards to integrate various video sources into a production workflow. While BlackMagic, Roland and other manufacturers have democratized access to professional video equipment, IP video has further-reaching implications for remote production. With technologies like NDI®, video sources can be captured directly through a computer's network interface, circumventing the need for costly hardware and enabling a more accessible approach to remote video production.

IP Video Implementation Considerations

While the benefits are substantial, transitioning to an IP video setup, particularly for remote production, does require consideration of certain challenges:

- **Networking Knowledge**: Those accustomed to conventional video standards may find the networking aspect of IP video daunting. While basic setups can be straightforward, more complex configurations demand a deeper understanding of

networking principles. Video professionals often add freelance or staff network engineers to their teams.
- **Infrastructure Requirements**: Implementing IP video for remote production may necessitate upgrades to existing network infrastructure to ensure sufficient bandwidth and reliability, critical for maintaining high-quality video streams across various locations.
- **Training and Support**: Adequate training in IP video and networking is crucial for teams to leverage the full potential of this technology.

Networking Infrastructure for Remote Production

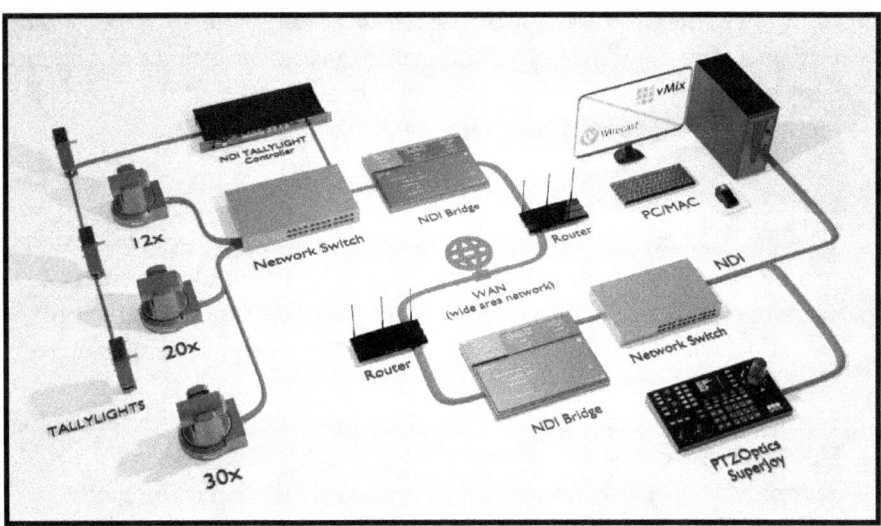

Three camera IP-video system with NDI bridge connecting the cameras to a remote camera operator.

This image above shows two Local Area Networks (LAN) connected together via a Wide Area Network (WAN) such as the Internet, using NDI Bridge. Each LAN has a Router which is connected to the network. Routers are generally provided by Internet Service Providers (ISP). Routers can be used to manage the devices on the LAN and your connection to the public internet. In this system, the remote camera operator is using a PTZOptics SuperJoy PTZ camera controller. The camera LAN is shown connected to a network switch on the client side of the NDI Bridge sending video to the far end.

Local Area Networks (LAN)

A Local Area Network (LAN) is crucial in a remote production setting as it connects all the local computing devices, such as computers, servers, and production equipment, within a limited area like a studio or production house. LANs are responsible for ensuring high-speed connections and the secure transfer of large video and audio files necessary for production within the local environment.

Wide Area Networks (WAN)

Unlike LANs, Wide Area Networks (WANs), like the internet itself connect devices over broader geographical areas. In remote production, WANs are essential for linking various production locations to central studios or cloud services. They facilitate the seamless transmission of multimedia content across cities or even continents, ensuring that remote teams can collaborate effectively regardless of distance.

Edge Devices

Edge devices play a pivotal role in managing data processing at or near the source of data acquisition. In remote productions, edge devices can process audio and video data before it travels over the network, significantly reducing latency and bandwidth usage. These devices can sit on the "edge" of networks and serve as a simple connection point to the cloud which can generally get around most firewall issues.

Remote Production

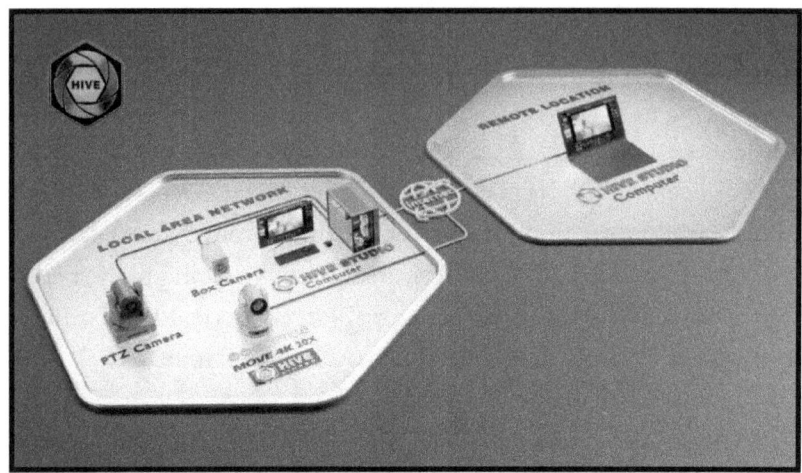

Diagram showing Hive Studio used to remotely control cameras. This diagram shows the difference between IP connected devices and edge devices.

Edge devices operate differently from normal IP-connected devices as shown in the diagram above. While the "PTZ Camera" and "Box Camera" are both connected to the LAN, they do not support a direct connection to the cloud and are therefore not edge devices. These devices require additional software to be connected to the cloud, which in this case is the Hive Studio client running on a computer on the same local area network. The Hive Studio software is able to act as a bridge for these IP connected devices and the cloud.

The camera at the bottom of the diagram is an edge device. This "Hive-Linked" PTZOptics camera can connect directly to the cloud without the need of a computer in the middle. This is ideal for deployments of multiple

REMOTE PRODUCTION
PRO TIP

PTZOptics Hive is free to use with one camera. You can learn more about this remote production software here.

devices on a network and remote productions that are looking to streamline their setup. Edge devices are often configured once, on a LAN by the owner of the device. This one time setup involves associating the device with the specific cloud account that it should connect to. For PTZOptics Hive-Linked cameras, this would involve accessing the camera interface, and logging into the Hive studio you would like the camera to be connected to.

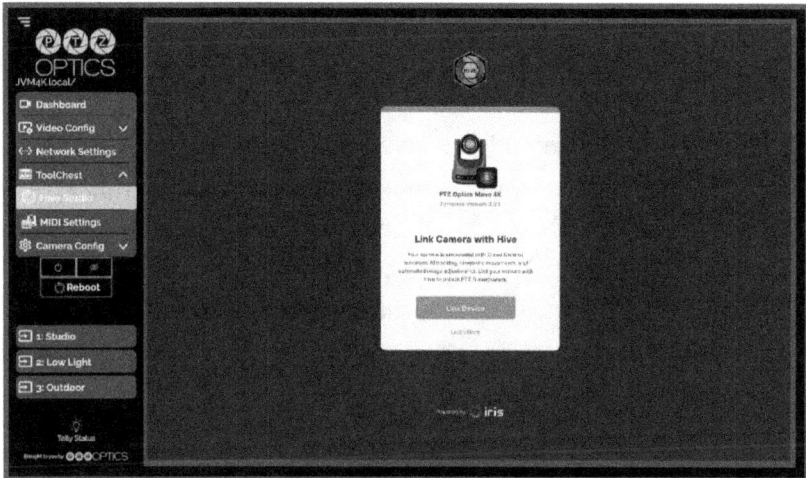

The web-interface for a PTZOptics Hive-Linked camera. This is how you can link a PTZOptics camera to a specific cloud studio.

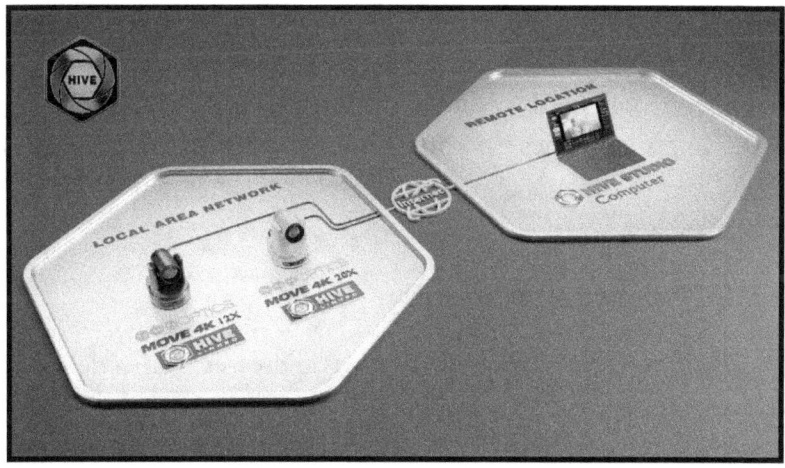

This diagram shows two PTZOptics Hive-Linked cameras connected for remote production.

VPNs and Firewalls

VPNs encrypt data traffic, creating secure connections between remote production sites and central studios over the internet. Firewalls provide an additional layer of security by blocking unauthorized access and monitoring network traffic to prevent and detect malicious activities. Edge devices are often used to get around firewall issues, , and they often play a crucial role in simplifying complex setups, allowing remote producers to integrate multiple network segments efficiently. By seamlessly connecting to the cloud, edge devices ensure that broadcasts are not compromised by firewalls in most cases. The strategic use of VPNs, firewalls, and edge devices collectively enhances the resilience of remote production workflows against potential cyber threats and technical challenges, ensuring smooth and secure operations across diverse geographic locations.

Static IP Addresses:

Static IP addresses are manually assigned to a device and remain constant unless changed by network administration. In remote production environments, static IPs are beneficial because they ensure that devices such as cameras, streaming servers, and production equipment consistently maintain the same address on the network. This predictability simplifies the configuration of networked devices, makes them easier to manage remotely, and reduces the potential for IP conflicts.

DHCP Assigned IP Addresses:

DHCP automates the assignment of IP addresses from a defined pool, which means that devices may receive a different IP address each time they connect to the network. This method is useful in dynamic environments where devices frequently join or leave the network, such as in temporary setups or locations with many mobile devices. DHCP simplifies the network management by reducing the administrative burden of manually assigning addresses. However, in a remote production setting, the lack of fixed IP addresses can lead to issues with device discovery and stream reliability, unless additional measures are implemented, such as DHCP reservation or dynamic DNS services to maintain continuity.

In summary, for remote production and IP video, static IP addresses are generally preferred due to their stability and predictability, which are essential for maintaining uninterrupted live video feeds and managing remote devices effectively. DHCP, while convenient for more dynamic or less critical network environments, may require additional configuration to meet the demands of remote production settings effectively.

Domain Name System (DNS) and Multicast DNS (mDNS)

The Domain Name System (DNS) and Multicast DNS (mDNS) are vital components of network communication, serving different but complementary functions. DNS is a hierarchical and decentralized system that translates human-friendly domain names into IP addresses necessary for network communication. This system is essential for accessing websites and services on the internet. For instance, when a URL is entered into a web browser, DNS servers resolve the domain name into an IP address, facilitating a connection to the desired server.

	DNS	mDNS
Scope	Global internet	Local networks

Operation	Hierarchical and decentralized	Zero-configuration networking within local scope
Function	Translates domain names into IP addresses for global internet access	Resolves hostnames to IP addresses without a central DNS server on local networks
Usage	Essential for accessing websites and services across the internet	Useful for service discovery and communication among devices on the same local network
Configuration	Requires configuration and maintenance of DNS servers	Does not require traditional DNS setup; operates seamlessly on the local network
Network Address	Uses specific DNS servers' IP addresses	Uses a multicast address to communicate directly among devices
Example Process	1. User enters URL in browser. 2. Query sent to DNS server. 3. Server returns IP address. 4. Connection established to website.	1. Device sends a multicast query on the local network. 2. Devices respond with IP addresses. 3. Direct communication established with local devices.

On the other hand, mDNS operates primarily within local networks to enable the discovery and communication of network services and devices without the need for a traditional DNS server. It supports zero-configuration networking by using a multicast address to resolve hostnames to IP addresses directly among local devices. This makes mDNS crucial for seamless network operations in environments without a dedicated DNS server.

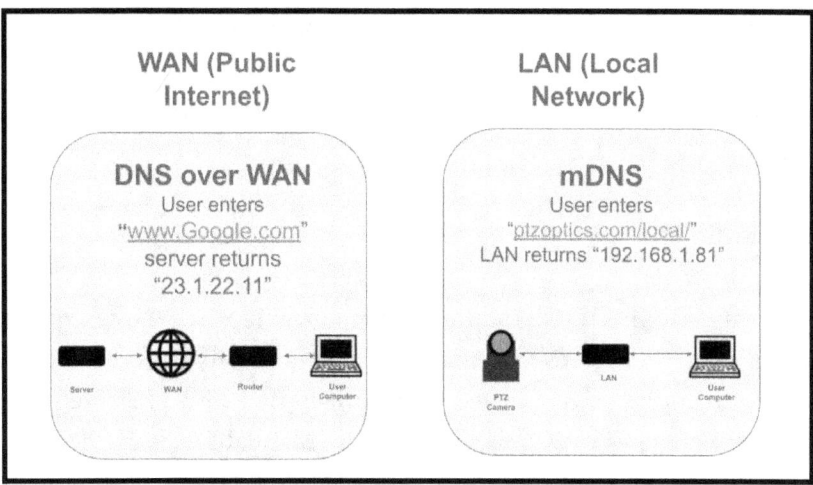

This diagram provides examples for DNS and mDNS.

Practical Example:

When a PTZOptics camera is first connected to a network, it typically acquires an IP address automatically from a DHCP server. This is standard for most network devices that are designed to operate seamlessly within existing infrastructures. Alongside this, the camera registers an mDNS address, which is 'PTZOptics.local`. This allows the camera to be easily identifiable and accessible within the local network without requiring users to remember or look up its dynamically assigned IP address. You can simply type "PTZOptics.local/" into any web browser and you can connect to the camera.

Once connected to the camera via its mDNS address, administrators have the option to modify its network settings. A common adjustment is changing the camera's IP setting from dynamic (DHCP) to a static IP address. Setting a static IP is particularly useful in production environments where devices need to remain accessible at consistent addresses. Transitioning to a static IP ensures that the camera can be reliably assessed at the same address, enhancing the stability and reliability of the network configuration.

Both DNS and mDNS are crucial for efficient network communication, with DNS facilitating global internet connectivity and mDNS enhancing local network service discovery and configuration. Understanding both systems is key to managing and troubleshooting network issues effectively.

Dynamic DNS

Dynamic DNS (DDNS) addresses the challenge posed by frequently changing IP addresses in dynamically assigned networks. In traditional DNS, IP addresses associated with domain names are relatively static, meaning changes in IP addresses require manual DNS updates.

DDNS automates this process by linking a domain name to a potentially frequently-changing IP address. This linkage is maintained through a DDNS service, such as NoIP.com, which monitors the IP address for changes and automatically updates the DNS records when changes occur. This seamless update process ensures that the domain name always points to the correct IP address, thereby maintaining connectivity and access without manual intervention.

Practical Application in Remote Production

While some Internet Service Providers (ISP) will provide a static outside IP address that can be used for remote production, many do not. A static outside IP address can be critical for sending and receiving video streams using SRT for example. If your ISP is unable to deliver you a static outside IP address, you can set up a Dynamic DNS service to have a known location to send video into your network. With a known address, you can configure your router to allow video via SRT for example to be received into your video production software from outside your network. Production of live events often requires that the central hub be located at the remote production's location. This means that the destination for other content feeds into the production will have a new physical location (and IP address) for this production. No-

Ip's Dynamic DNS Update Client continually checks for IP address changes in the background and automatically updates the DNS at No-IP whenever it changes, so you don't have to change your destination's hostname.

Benefits of DDNS

1. **Continuous Accessibility**: Devices remain accessible via the same hostname even as their IP addresses change, which is crucial for remote monitoring and management of production equipment.
2. **Cost Efficiency**: Reduces the need for static IP addresses, which are often more expensive and less scalable than dynamic IP addresses provided by ISPs.
3. **Enhanced Security**: By using domain names, DDNS adds a layer of obfuscation to device IP addresses, potentially reducing vulnerability to network scanning and attacks.

Understanding DDNS is key for professionals managing remote production environments, where maintaining constant and secure connections to various devices is crucial. By automating IP address updates in DNS records, DDNS ensures that domain names reliably direct to the appropriate devices, despite any changes in their IP addresses. This dynamic approach not only improves operational efficiency but also enhances the overall stability of network communications in remote productions.

Dynamic Host Configuration Protocol (DHCP)

In the context of remote production and IP video, the choice between using static IP addresses and DHCP (Dynamic Host Configuration Protocol) assigned IP addresses can significantly impact network management and device reliability. In general, DHCP should be used for the connection of devices that are used temporarily, such as a smartphone or a tablet. Static IP addresses should be used for permanently installed devices such as cameras, encoders and IP controllers.

Bridging Data Between Two LANs

Connecting two Local Area Networks (LANs) involves bridging them to allow seamless data and resource sharing. This is often achieved through technologies such as VPNs or specialized video transport protocols such as SRT which require port forwarding. The first time I experienced connecting two LANs together was through testing the NDI Bridge. The NDI Bridge is a free NDI tool which can be used with an outside IP address using their client and host software. Once connected I was able to view and control a PTZ camera from the far end of the LAN managing a buffer for the video.

One simple way to "remote" into a network from a remote location is by a remote computer management software such as TeamViewer or Parsec. This software allows you to gain control over a computer which already has access to the local network and other devices such as cameras and audio mixers.

For example assume you are in charge of recording an important business meeting using remote video production capabilities. You have two PTZOptics NDI cameras, vMix software, Parsec for remote access, and Zoom Webinar where the live meeting will take place.

Scenario: Remote Production for a Corporate Business Meeting

Setup:

Camera and Network Configuration: The video production team sends two PTZOptics NDI cameras to the meeting location. These cameras are set to receive IP addresses from the DHCP server, and will be controlled over the network by vMix. The cameras are set up at strategic locations to capture different angles of the meeting room.

Local Computer Setup: A computer installed with vMix is ready on the local area network at the meeting site. This computer is configured to handle live mixing, recording, and streaming of video feeds.

Remote Access via Parsec: Parsec is installed on the same computer to enable remote access. The video production team remotely logs into this computer from their location. Parsec is selected for its low latency and high-quality video streaming capabilities, which are crucial for managing live video feeds effectively.

Execution:

Pre-Meeting Checks: Before the meeting starts, the remote video production team logs in through Parsec to configure vMix settings. They check the camera positions and movements using PTZ controls, adjust audio levels, and prepare graphic overlays like lower thirds that will display participant names and titles.

During the Meeting: As the meeting progresses, the team switches between cameras to focus on the current speaker, utilizes zoom features for close-ups, and dynamically changes lower thirds as different participants speak. All these controls are managed through the vMix interface on the remote desktop.

Zoom Webinar Integration: The output from vMix is fed directly into a Zoom Webinar using the virtual webcam output. This setup allows online meeting participants to view the professionally produced video stream, complete with live switching and graphics, as if it were a broadcast-quality production.

Benefits:

Professional Production Quality: Leveraging PTZOptics cameras and vMix software enhances the production value of the business meeting, making it engaging for remote viewers.

Efficiency and Flexibility: Remote control via Parsec allows the production team to manage the event from anywhere, reducing the need for travel and onsite technical staff.

Enhanced Interactivity: By using Zoom Webinar, the meeting can reach a broader audience, include interactive elements like Q&A sessions, and utilize Zoom's robust platform features to manage audience engagement.

Alternative Solutions

Remote PTZ Control via Zoom: PTZOptics USB connected cameras can be controlled via Zoom on the far end. This can be done by requesting PTZ camera control access from the far end. One issue is that a person on the far end needs to approve access to the camera.

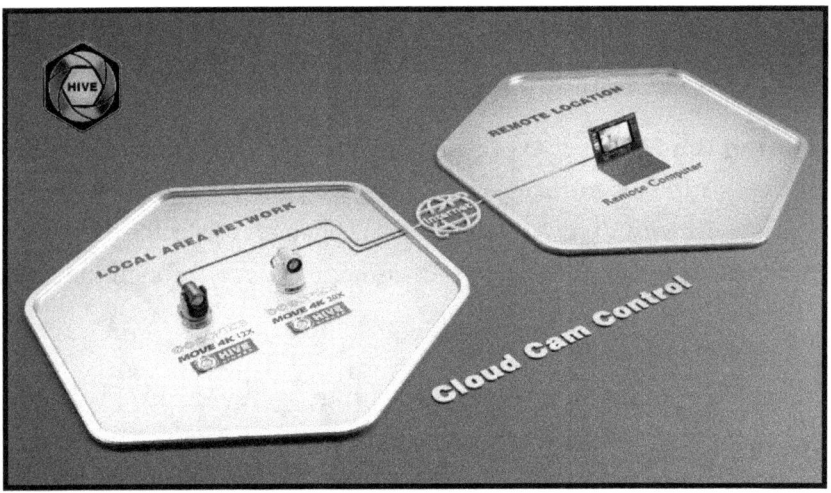

This diagram shows a remote location controlling two Hive-Linked PTZOptics cameras on the far end.

Hive-Connected PTZ Cameras: Using PTOptics Hive the production team can remotely control the cameras without the need for a computer on the far end. They can simply connect their Hive-Linked PTZ cameras to their studio and once those PTZ cameras are connected to the internet, they will be available for remote control in the production team's Hive Studio.

NDI Bridge: If you are the IT administrator or are able to do port-forwarding on the network router, NDI Bridge can be used to connect to the NDI cameras on the far end of the video production. NDI Bridge requires a host and a client running on a Windows or Mac computer. Once set up the two LANs are connected and can be used for sending and receiving video. The nice thing about NDI is that it can also be used for PTZ control.

Most NDI users start their journey with NDI by seeking a new way of connecting video sources beyond the traditional HDMI and SDI cable types. Getting started can be as easy as downloading the free NDI tools. Over the years, NDI tools have grown to include NDI viewing applications, screen capture software, virtual webcams inputs, and remote camera control options. There are even apps for iOS and Android that can turn your smartphone into a camera or presentation tool. NDI Tools allow anyone to get started using IP video and easily leapfrog old technologies that used to require expensive capture cards and hardware video switchers.

Luckily, little networking knowledge is required to start using NDI. If you use OBS, it's simple, just download the NDI plugin and start sharing the output of your OBS production on your network with another computer. If you use vMix, try searching for NDI sources on your network that you might want to incorporate into your production, like a smartphone with the NDI app running. There are so many ways to use NDI with thousands of software and hardware configurations.

KEY TAKEAWAYS FROM THIS CHAPTER:

1. IP Video Fundamentals:
    - IP Video utilizes network protocols to manage and distribute video over IP networks, revolutionizing remote production with increased scalability and efficiency.

2. Networking in Remote Production:

    - Local Area Networks (LANs): Essential for connecting local devices within a studio or production site, facilitating high-speed, secure data transfers.

    - Wide Area Networks (WANs): Connects devices across larger geographical areas, enabling remote teams to collaborate and share multimedia content seamlessly.

    - Edge Devices: Process data at or near the source, reducing latency and bandwidth usage, crucial for efficient remote productions.

    - Security and Management: VPNs and firewalls ensure secure, reliable connections across networks, while DNS and mDNS manage network communications effectively.

8 ZOOM FOR REMOTE PRODUCTION

Few video meeting companies have provided the same level of professional broadcast features as Zoom. Zoom has gone above and beyond, through feature releases, new product launches and acquisitions, to cater to the broadcast market. The Zoom Events platform is a prime example of Zoom's presence in the virtual events space. Zoom's acquisition of Liminal, the creators of ZoomISO is another. Zoom has become a primary tool for broadcasters working on podcasts, talk shows and other remote guest situations. Therefore, this chapter is dedicated to valuable tools available to broadcasters in the ecosystem.

Here's are a few key Zoom feature for Remote Production:

1. **Direct Streaming Integration**: Zoom Meetings and Webinars can be directly streamed to YouTube, Facebook, or any custom Content Delivery Network (CDN), facilitating live broadcasts to a wide audience without needing complex setups.

2. **NDI Output:** With Zoom Rooms and Zoom ISO, video sources can be outputted via NDI, allowing seamless integration into larger production workflows. This feature enables professional-quality video and audio sources to be incorporated into more extensive broadcast environments.

3. **Preparation Tools for Guests**: Zoom provides waiting-room functionalities; including "breakout rooms" that are particularly useful for prepping guests before they go into a meeting or webinar that is being live streamed. This feature helps in managing participants and ensuring a smooth transition to live sessions.

4. **Comprehensive Event Platform**: Zoom Events integrates the capabilities of Zoom Meetings and Webinars into a robust

virtual event platform. This service simplifies hosting complex events involving multiple sessions and tracks, offering tools for both live and pre-recorded segments.

These features make Zoom an adaptable tool for enhancing broadcast and streaming production, ensuring high-quality outputs and efficient management of live interactions.

Capturing a Zoom Meeting

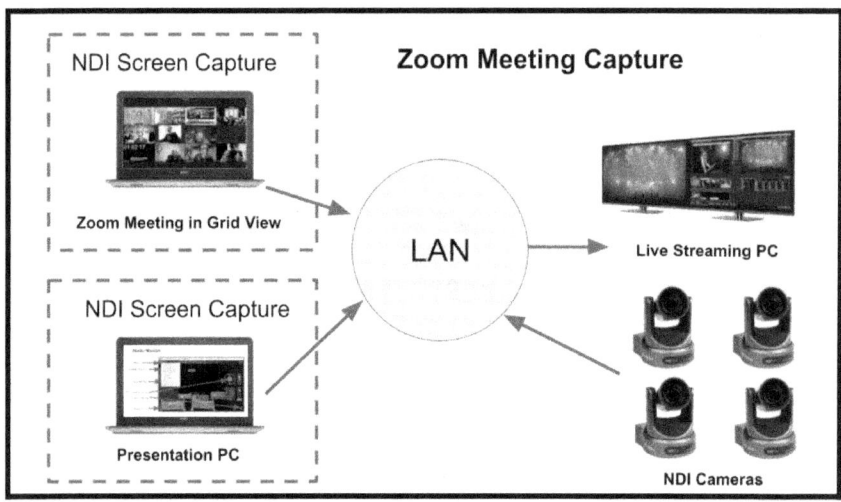

NDI Screen Capture and a few more NDI cameras.

Capturing a video from a Zoom meeting can be done in several ways. A screen capture solution with your video production software might be the easiest way, but you have multiple options to choose from depending on your workflow. It's important to note that in order to gain 1080p video quality, you will need to use a Zoom Professional account and have the 1080p video option enabled.

Those who work with Zoom should be aware of Zoom ISO which can separate each participant's video feed into its own video output. This is particularly useful for professional video productions and broadcasts, where a director might want to manage individual feeds separately. Additionally, Zoom ISO can output each video feed via NDI to be integrated into any production software that supports NDI.

When you are working with Zoom, you may want to consider sending a "reference" video feed back into Zoom for meeting participants to see your production. You can use the NDI Webcam Input to bring NDI video back into Zoom via a virtual webcam. To take this NDI Zoom capture project one step further, you can see the next diagram includes two different video capture methods in the same Zoom meeting. How is this possible? Using multiple computers, the StreamGeeks will often connect to the same Zoom meeting to display the content in various ways.

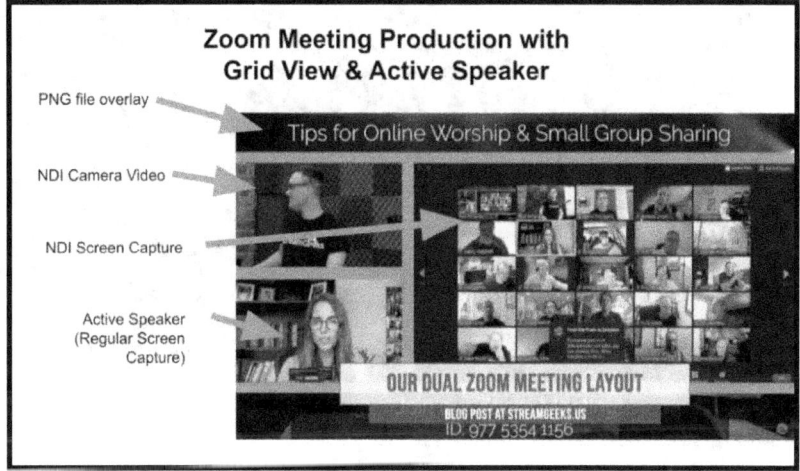

A Zoom meeting with an active speaker alongside the Grid View built from NDI video sources.

During certain live streams, it's nice to be able to show the active speaker in a larger window. And as a producer, it's good to have the active speaker in the Zoom meeting available as its own input to appear in a full screen. Here you can see the active speaker is actually shown in a regular screen capture. This means that vMix, or another type of software, is simply capturing a screen that is connected to the computer directly without NDI. While this does take up precious monitor space, the StreamGeeks will often use NDI on a separate computer to capture the active speaker view.

Understanding ZoomISO

ZoomISO is a valuable remote production solution from Zoom made specifically for remote contribution and broadcasting. This macOS-based application enhances Zoom's capabilities by offering flexible video management and control options.

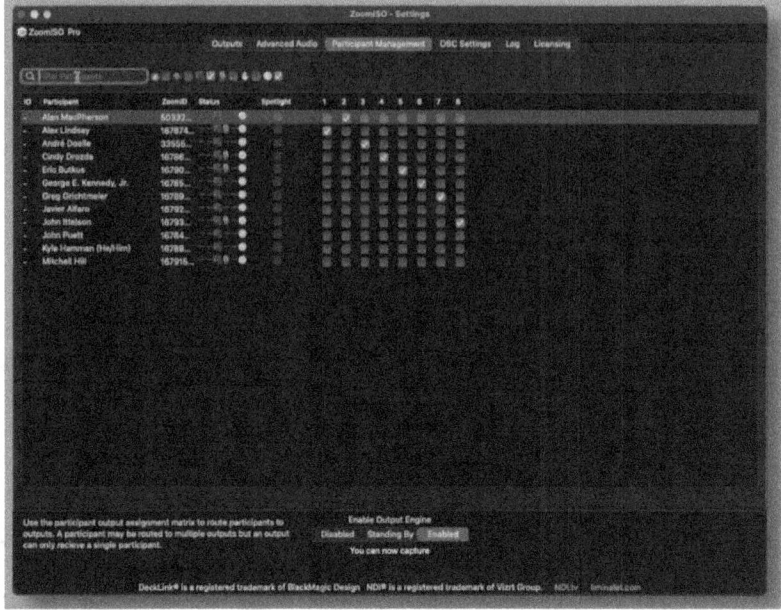

ZoomISO showing the participant management tab.

ZoomISO allows for individual Zoom participants to be exported as isolated video outputs, making it ideal for productions that require separate feeds of each participant. It supports a variety of output formats compatible with mainstream production systems, such as NDI 5, Metal Syphon, SRT, and SDI through Blackmagic Desktop Video. Outputs can be assigned not only to these video technologies but also to multiple display options including Physical Displays and DisplayLink.

The application can export video feeds in HD quality, provided the Zoom Meeting or Webinar supports HD video. Audio feeds can be embedded in the video outputs or managed independently. ZoomISO supports various audio tools including Dante Virtual Soundcard, Loopback, and Black Hole, allowing for flexible audio routing and integration into broader production setups.

The application can be controlled remotely via Open Sound Control (OSC), facilitating complex feed routing. This feature is particularly useful when using devices like a Stream Deck to manage feeds dynamically during live production.

ZoomISO is designed to streamline the production workflow by replacing the need for multiple "pinning machines"—setups where multiple laptops screen scrape individual users into production software like vMix. A single instance of ZoomISO running on a macOS machine can replace several Windows-based pinning setups, offering a more consolidated and flexible approach to vision mixing.

It is recommended to use dedicated hardware for specific tasks to prevent resource conflicts. For instance, having a dedicated macOS computer for ZoomISO to handle decoding, while a separate Windows machine manages encoding and vision mixing tasks ensures efficiency and stability in production workflows. With ZoomISO, production teams can achieve higher flexibility and quality in handling remote contributions, enhancing their capability to produce dynamic and engaging live broadcasts and events.

ZoomISO Lite is capable of exporting up to 4 video feeds. In contrast, ZoomISO Pro features a "high bandwidth mode" that utilizes additional bandwidth from the Zoom Cloud to support more outputs. The capacity of ZoomISO Pro to export additional participant video feeds depends on maintaining system utilization below 80% and ensuring the network WAN link to the Zoom Cloud does not exceed 100mb/s. Each 1080p video feed from Zoom typically requires 4-6 mb/s.

Exceeding the network bandwidth limit could lead to throttled frame rates, while surpassing the system utilization limit might result in Zoom sending a lower resolution video feed to ZoomISO. This could trigger additional scaling processes, potentially increasing CPU usage, and possibly forcing a reduction in resolution to 360p to maintain stable CPU utilization. It's important to note that not all Zoom meetings support HD; this capability must be enabled by Zoom support and activated in the user interface. Regardless of the input resolution from the Zoom Cloud, ZoomISO always strives to output the specified resolution and frame timings, employing upscaling, downscaling, or frame adjustment as necessary. For detailed benchmarks and further information, users are encouraged to refer to the Liminal website.

Beginning with version 27, Vmix connects with the Zoom API and can bring Zoom participants into Vmix in much the same way that Zoom Iso does; as individual video feeds with individual audio. While not as robust as Zoom Iso, Vmix runs on a Windows PC and doesn't require an additional computer for Zoom integration.

ZoomOSC

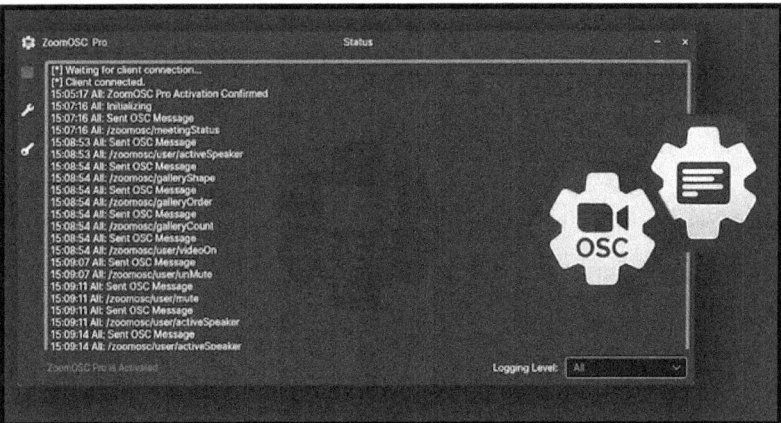

ZoomOSC Pro showing real time OSC messaging.

ZoomOSC is an advanced version of the Zoom client designed to enhance the management and control of virtual meetings and events by integrating with third-party software and hardware via the Open Sound Control (OSC) protocol. ZoomOSC is now available for both Mac and PC computers. This tool elevates, automates, and streamlines virtual events by enabling OSC to send commands to control various Zoom functions such as pinning, spotlighting, video toggling, and screen sharing. Additionally, ZoomOSC outputs real-time data for meeting status, participant information, gallery positions, and chat messages, which can be utilized to create custom control surfaces for Zoom using OSC-compatible hardware controllers or applications.

ZoomOSC is particularly valuable for broadcasters, theaters, content creators, and anyone involved in producing virtual events and interactive experiences. The software facilitates complex event sequences with features like multi-pinning and spotlighting, allowing users to execute precise participant management and control with simple button presses. This capability enhances the reliability and dynamism of productions, making it possible to manage complicated sequences easily.

The user interface of ZoomOSC is designed to be intuitive and accessible, making it easy for non-programmers to use. Users can adjust application IP and port settings for compatibility and customize their control surfaces to fit into their specific workflow needs. Enhanced output features in ZoomOSC provide detailed feedback about participant actions and meeting dynamics, enabling integrators to drive functions based on real-time data. These features collectively empower users to create sophisticated and highly interactive virtual event environments without the need for extensive programming knowledge.

Tiles

Tiles for Zoom is an innovative macOS application developed by Liminal, designed to transform how Zoom audience galleries are customized and displayed, particularly for hybrid event auditoriums and live streams. This application offers a user-friendly editor interface that allows for the simple composition of Zoom participants onto customizable gallery canvases. These galleries can then be exported to various production protocols, enhancing the integration with professional broadcasting tools.

The Zoom Tiles interface allows users to mix and match video sources into a unique view.

The core feature of Tiles is its deep customization capabilities. Users can design their Zoom audience galleries with precision, setting any canvas dimension and customizing tile layouts to fit the specific needs of their event. The design features include custom borders, rounded corners, aspect ratios, drop shadows, and transparency effects, all of which can be adjusted to create the perfect look and feel. Additionally, Tiles offers live pre-visualization, allowing users to see and tweak how their galleries will appear with different audience sizes in real time. This feature is complemented by the ability to set rules for animations and layout changes based on the gallery audience dynamics.

Organizing participants is streamlined with Tiles' robust moderation tools. Users can filter participants to display only those who are necessary, with options to favorite or block participants, sort them by roles or video status, and set rules to exclude non-video participants or other specific user categories. There is also a participant rotation queue feature, which automatically replaces participants displayed in the galleries to ensure everyone in the meeting is featured.

In beta as of this writing, Tiles supports exporting galleries to NDI, facilitating easy connectivity with other hardware or software on the network. The developers plan to support additional production protocols in future updates, which will further enhance its utility in professional settings. Tiles is available through the Zoom App Marketplace, and while the free trial version offers full functionality, it does not allow users to join Zoom Meetings or Webinars. Full functionality, including the ability to join any Zoom Meeting, Webinar, or Event—even those outside the Zoom Events platform or owned by other Zoom accounts— requires a licensed activation. This is available to accounts that are designated as Hub Hosts through the Zoom Events platform, with the number of available Hub Hosts depending on the Zoom Events or Zoom Session license purchased.

Tiles for Zoom promises to be a significant asset for broadcasters, event organizers, and content creators who are looking to elevate, automate, and streamline their virtual events with professionally styled and highly interactive audience galleries. The application is set to be available soon on the Zoom Events platform, and interested users can sign up for the newsletter to be notified when the beta is available for download.

REMOTE PRODUCTION PRO TIP

The Liminal website outlines the technical deails for ZoomISO, ZoomOSC and Tiles.

KEY TAKEAWAYS FROM THIS CHAPTER:

1. **Advanced Broadcast Features**: Zoom has established itself as a leader in professional broadcast features compared to other video meeting platforms. This is evident through its continuous updates, product launches, and strategic acquisitions aimed at enhancing its offerings for the broadcast market.

2. **Zoom Events Platform**: As a standout example, Zoom Events showcases Zoom's commitment to the virtual events space, providing a comprehensive platform for hosting complex, multi-track events with both live and pre-recorded content.
3. **Acquisition of Liminal**: The acquisition of Liminal, the creators of ZoomISO, underscores Zoom's focus on catering to broadcasters, especially in settings like podcasts and talk shows where high-quality video and audio are crucial.
4. **The Zoom API:** Integrations with Zoom via its Application Programming Interface (API) allows production platforms like Vmix to bring individual participant video and audio to their programs.
5. **Direct Streaming Integration**: This feature allows Zoom Meetings and Webinars to be directly streamed to platforms like YouTube, Facebook, or any custom CDN, facilitating broad distribution without the need for complex setups.
6. **NDI Output**: Available in Zoom Rooms and through Zoom ISO, this feature supports seamless integration of Zoom's video sources into larger, professional broadcast workflows by outputting video via NDI (Network Device Interface).
7. **Preparation Tools for Guests**: Features like waiting rooms are particularly useful for preparing guests before they enter live-streamed meetings or webinars, ensuring smooth transitions and well-managed participant interactions.
8. **ZoomISO and ZoomOSC**: These tools are tailored for enhanced video management and virtual event control. ZoomISO provides flexible video control on macOS, while ZoomOSC integrates with third-party software and hardware via the OSC protocol, enhancing control over virtual meetings and events.

9 NETWORKING BASICS FOR REMOTE PRODUCTION

Using common network setups, IP video technologies such as NDI, RTSP, SRT, and Dante AV-H can enhance your ability to produce content remotely. Whether you're managing IP video remotely through software or streaming all your video signals to the cloud for production, having some knowledge of IP networking will be beneficial.

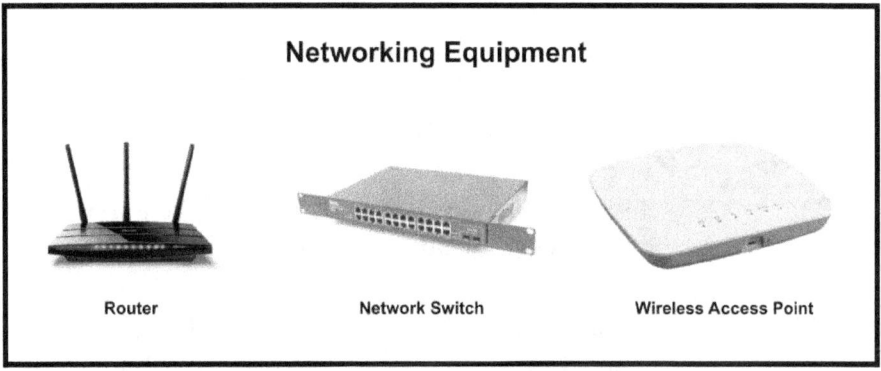

Common types of networking equipment.

A router is a common type of networking equipment which provides a safe communication space for computers connected to the network to access the internet. The rules of the LAN are generally managed by the router which has management pages that can be accessed securely by a computer on the network. The router manages the other computers and devices on the network and can even give devices IP addresses automatically using a protocol called Dynamic Host Configuration Protocol (DHCP). Some routers include a built-in network switch, but most are connected to a larger network switch which provides connectivity between all of the devices on the network. Some routers include WiFi connectivity with a built-in Wireless Access Point (WAP). Many networks distribute WAPs throughout an area to provide WiFi connectivity throughout a large space. Each WAP should be connected to the network with ethernet cables and many are Power Over Ethernet

(PoE, PoE+ or PoE++) capable; the "+" designations indicating higher available wattage. A PoE device can be powered by PoE enabled networking equipment using standard ethernet cables.

Below is an example of an IP address table. It's important that you are organized when it comes to managing the 254 IP addresses available on a single IP range, in order to effectively manage your LAN.

IP Address	Address Description
192.168.1.0	This is the first network number that identifies the network as a whole.
192.168.1.1	Number one is generally assigned to the router
192.168.1.2-254	These addresses may be assigned to devices on your network.
192.168.1.255	This is the broadcast address. Anything sent to this address is automatically broadcast to IP addresses 1-254.
21.233.221.1	This is an example of an outside IP address. An outside IP address is given to you by your Internet Service Provider (ISP).

The starting numbers can vary depending on how the network is set up.

Besides the computers and devices that are a part of the network, LANs require additional hardware to keep everything connected. In a home or small office, the network may be managed by a single router. ISPs often provide multipurpose all-in-one routers that offer access to the internet (via cable, fiber, or other connection). They also provide a wired and/or wireless network connection that enables connected devices to communicate with the internet and other devices on the LAN. Larger and more robust LANs may require additional hardware such as routers, switches, firewalls, and wireless access points. Professional-grade equipment at this level allows for more devices, better security, and network management.

In some situations, the network administrator can prioritize video traffic to reduce latency and avoid issues when there is too much traffic on the network. You may need to set up your own network for use specifically with IP video. It's possible to connect a computer to multiple LANs at the same time. This is easy to do if your computer has two Network Interface Cards (NICs). If your computer only has one NIC, you can purchase a USB to ethernet adapter to add an additional NIC port to your computer. Adding an additional NIC port will increase the amount of bandwidth your computer can access. Because NDI can load balance multiple NIC cards on a computer, this is an easy way to increase the amount of NDI sources you can use for your video production.

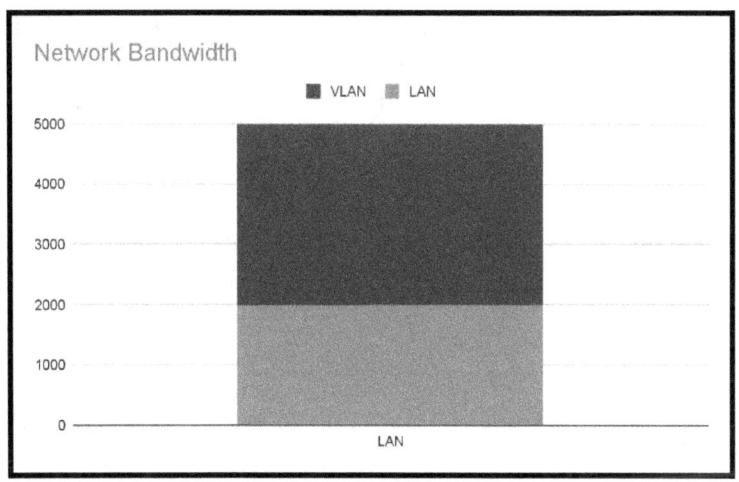

This example LAN shows bandwidth partitioning for a VLAN.

A virtual LAN (VLAN) can be used to set up a segmented part of a network specifically for IP video. Network administrators can set up a VLAN to partition resources inside of a larger LAN and provide additional reliability and security. VLANs are ideal for limiting network access to specific computers and devices. A VLAN is ideal for video traffic because you can reduce network traffic and the potential for packet collisions. Most networking equipment allows you to create a large number of VLANs. Each VLAN can be set up with access to specific resources on the network.

House of Worship Example

The following example will outline a video production network setup for a house of worship. For this example, a part of the network has been segmented for devices that are used for video production such as cameras and computers running video production software. Each device on the network has an IP address and in general, there are two different ways that you can assign devices IP addresses. They can be assigned a static IP address manually, or a dynamic IP address automatically. Static IP addresses never change, and therefore they are much better for managing an IP address table on your network. Dynamic IP addresses are assigned by your router using Dynamic Host Configuration Protocol (DHCP). This protocol is ideal for devices that periodically connect and disconnect from your network. A smartphone is a prime example of an IP-connected device that uses DHCP. When your smartphone connects to WiFi, it automatically gets an IP address from the network. It's a best practice to assign static IP addresses to the most important devices on your network used for video production. It's especially important to use a static IP address for devices like PTZ cameras that are permanently installed on your network.

Without getting too far into networking jargon, you can have up to 254 devices on a single network which can all communicate on the same IP range.

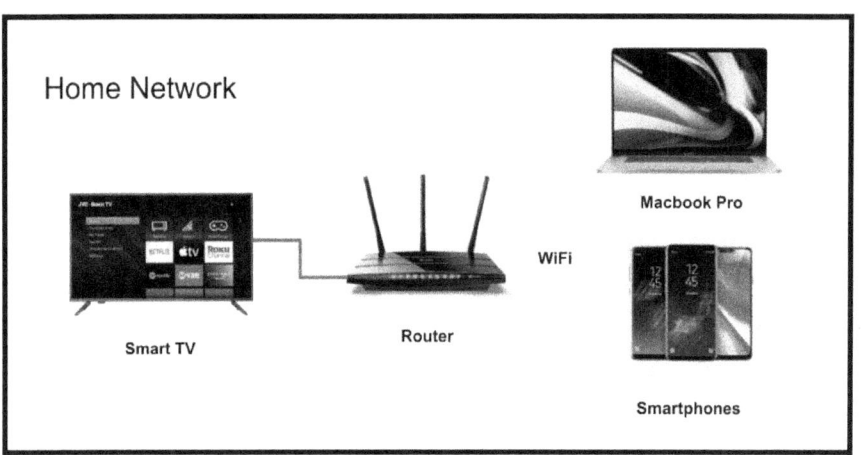

Home networks don't generally require a lot of networking hardware.

A simple home network like the one above uses a router provided by an ISP. This router includes a built-in network switch, a firewall, and a WiFi access point. A router like this will allow you to connect a few devices to your network right away such as a smart TV, smartphone, and a few computers. All-in-one routers are becoming more popular and affordable and can also be used with NDI®.

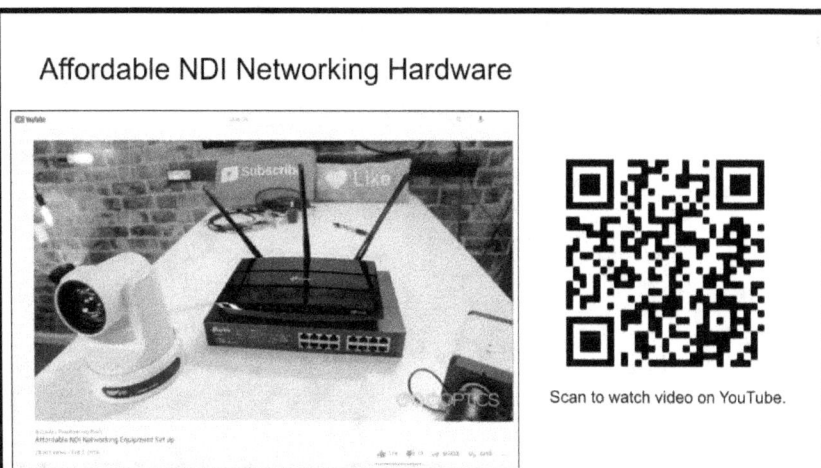

Affordable NDI® networking equipment set-up video on YouTube.

One popular networking set-up for NDI comes from TP-LINK. The StreamGeeks tested the TP-LINK Archer series of routers for use with NDI®. This "All-In-One" wireless router offers specific settings that work with multicast and IPTV for video routing. You can scan the QR code above or watch the video in a forthcoming online course to learn more about this set up. Even if you end up using different networking equipment, the six-minute video outlines all the steps required for most routers to be optimized for NDI.

Note: If you plan to power cameras and other devices using ethernet cables, you will want to purchase a network switch that supports Power Over Ethernet (PoE).

The next diagram shows that each device on the network is connected to a network switch. This network switch has PoE connectivity and it can power small devices such as PTZ cameras and joystick controllers.

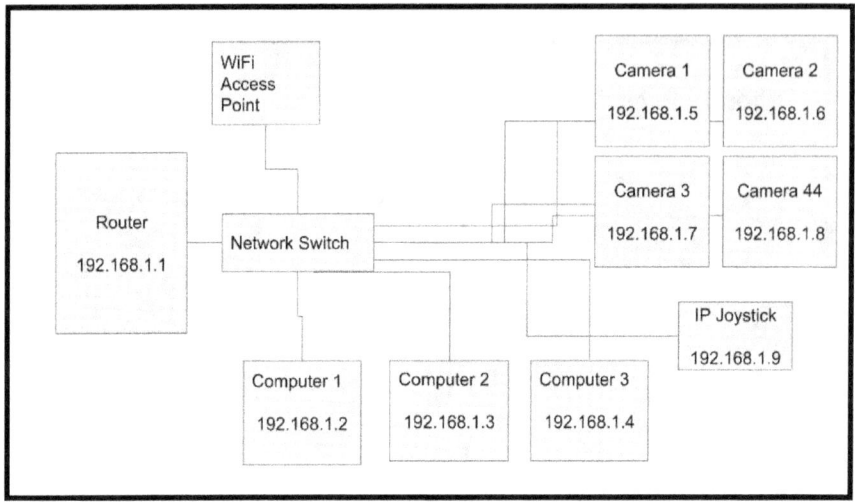

High-level networking diagram with IP addresses for each device.

The table below is helpful for referencing IP addresses when you need them. For example, if a PTZ camera is controllable with your video production software, the camera's unique IP address is often necessary to control it. Some software with web-server capabilities will use a port number to create a unique address for the software running on the network-connected computer. For example, if your main live streaming computer is running vMix, you may be using the vMix Social application which is controlled by a web-browser interface. If the computer's IP address is 192.168.1.70, vMix will automatically use port 8089 on the same base IP address to create a unique address to control vMix Social. Therefore, the IP address 192.168.1.70:8089 would open the controls for vMix Social.

IP Address	Device
192.168.1.0	Network Address
192.168.1.1	Router supplied by your Internet Service Provider
192.168.1.2-59	Used for office devices like office computers, printers, access points, and other IP connected devices
192.168.1.60	PTZOptics 20X - Main Camera in back of Church

192.168.1.61	PTZOptics 12X - Front Camera on Choir Area
192.168.1.62	PTZOptics 12X - Side Camera to on Stage
192.168.1.63	PTZOptics 30X - 2nd Camera in back of Church for Close Up Views
192.168.1.64	PTZOptics ZCam - Static Camera used for Drum Cage
192.168.1.65	PTZOptics ZCam - Static Camera used for Backstage
192.168.1.66	PTZOptics IP Joystick Controller
192.168.1.70	Main vMix Live Streaming Computer
192.168.1.70:8089	vMix Social Management Server
192.168.1.71	Pastor's on-Stage Laptop
192.168.1.72	Computer Powering 2 Displays in Lobby using NDI® Studio Monitor
192.168.1.73	Computer Powering 2 Displays in Nursery using NDI® Studio Monitor
192.168.1.74	Computer Powering 2 Displays on Stage for Confidence Monitoring
192.168.1.119*	iPad using NDI® Camera App (Wireless Camera)
192.168.1.123*	Smartphone used for iOS camera control app
*Assigned with DHCP	

The great thing about IP-based video production for so many users is that you likely already have a network in place at home. Thinking about your home network may help you make sense of the chart above. You may open up a whole new universe of possibilities where your existing network becomes the preferred method of video routing across your facility.

Need another camera shot? Just run a Cat-5e or better) cable to the camera. This single cable will give you high-quality video, a camera you can remotely control, and power for that camera in a single stroke. Want to send PowerPoint slides from a computer onstage back to the video production computer? No problem, everything is connected to the same network. Try using your home network with the NDI mobile app on your phone and see how easy it is to send video from your smartphone to your computer connected on the same network.

Once you have your LAN set up the way you want, it's very easy to transition this workflow for a remote production. The PTZOptics Hive software, for example, is able to search the local area network and connect each source to the cloud for remote production. Once the Hive software is installed on a computer on the LAN, each source you connect to your studio can be connected to the cloud for sharing with others on your team. Many studios use both local and remote access options that are available in Hive. This is why there is a Local/Cloud toggle at the top of the interface. This allows you to quickly view your connection type and if you want, temporarily "lock" the studio into local only mode. This will stop other users from accessing the local sources on the network, even if you have shared access with them.

KEY TAKEAWAYS FROM THIS CHAPTER:

1. **Importance of IP Video Technologies**: Technologies like NDI, RTSP, SRT, and Dante AV-H are crucial for enhancing remote content production capabilities. They allow for the efficient management and streaming of IP video signals, which are vital in modern broadcasting environments.

2. **Understanding IP Networking**: Gaining some knowledge of IP networking is beneficial as it supports the effective use of IP video technologies. This knowledge helps in optimizing network setups for remote production.

3. **Role of Routers**: Routers play a central role in network management. They provide internet access, manage LAN rules, and can automatically assign IP addresses using DHCP. Some routers also include built-in network switches or Wi-Fi capabilities, enhancing network connectivity.

4. **Use of Wireless Access Points (WAPs)**: WAPs are distributed across areas to extend Wi-Fi coverage. They are

often connected via Ethernet and many support Power Over Ethernet (PoE), allowing them to receive power through network cables from PoE-enabled equipment.

5. **Benefits of VLANs**: Virtual LANs (VLANs) are used to create segmented parts of a network, ideal for IP video to reduce traffic and prevent packet collisions. VLANs improve network security and efficiency by limiting access to network resources to specific devices.

6. **Network Configuration for Video Traffic**: Setting up a VLAN specifically for video traffic helps in managing bandwidth and enhances the reliability of video streaming within a network.

7. **Remote Production Software**: Software solutions like PTZOptics Hive facilitate the integration of local video sources with cloud-based production platforms. This software can identify and connect networked video sources for remote access and collaboration.

8. **Local and Cloud Access:** Studios often toggle between local and cloud access to manage how video sources are shared and accessed within the network. Features like a Local/Cloud toggle help in quickly switching the operational mode of the studio, providing control over local sources and preventing unauthorized remote access.

10 Optimizing for Bandwidth

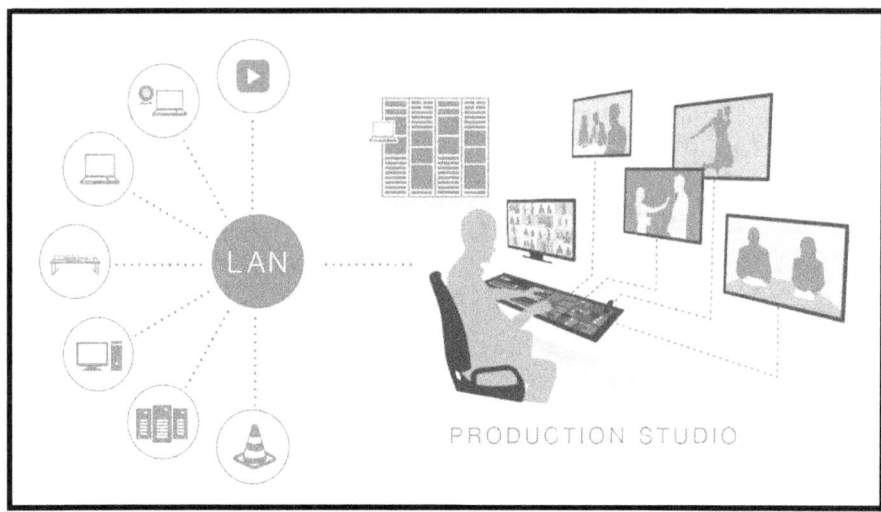

A modern video production system connected to a Local Area Network (LAN).

The main bottleneck most IP video users confront is a limitation of bandwidth. In video production you will deal with limitations on the network infrastructure and limitations from your ISP. In remote production, you should always have an idea of the bandwidth your production requires and the headroom you are leaving for flexibility.

WAN Bandwidth Considerations

Technology Type	Typical Speed Range	Suitable Resolutions	Equipment Needed	Notes
3G	384 Kbps - 2 Mbps	Up to 480p	Mobile device, modem	Least reliable, phased out

Connection	Speed	Resolution	Equipment	Notes
Basic DSL	1-5 Mbps	480p - 720p	DSL modem	Limited availability
4G LTE	5-30 Mbps	720p - 1080p	Mobile device, modem	Widely available
5G	50 Mbps - 1 Gbps	720p - 4K	5G enabled devices	Widely available
WiFi	10-100+ Mbps	720p - 4K	Router, wireless NIC	Subject to interference
Ethernet	100 Mbps - 1 Gbps	720p - 4K	Ethernet cables, ports	Most stable connection
Cellular Bonding	Varies	720p - 4K	Bonding device	Enhanced reliability
Multiple-SIM Cards	Varies	720p - 4K	Multi-SIM device	Enhanced reliability

Upload speeds are crucial, as they determine the resolution and stability of your remote production. Connections range from older 3G mobile data, which can handle up to 480p resolution at speeds between 384 Kbps to 2 Mbps, to modern 5G networks that boast speeds from 50 Mbps to 1 Gbps, enabling high-definition and ultra-high-definition streaming. Intermediate options like 4G LTE offer reliable 720p to

1080p streaming at 5-30 Mbps, suitable for most mobile streaming scenarios.

For fixed internet options, Ethernet provides the most stable connection with speeds typically ranging from 100 Mbps to 1 Gbps, ideal for professional setups requiring the highest video quality. WiFi, while broadly available, may suffer from interference, making it less reliable for professional uses despite supporting speeds up to 100+ Mbps. Advanced techniques like cellular bonding and routers with multiple-SIM cards enhance connectivity and failover capabilities, making them valuable for high-stakes live reporting and events where connection disruption can easily be a problem.

LAN Bandwidth Considerations

You should always have a strong understanding of the bandwidth available on your LAN. Four areas where bandwidth can be limited include the cabling you use, the networking equipment (router, switch, or wireless access point), the Network Interface Card (NIC) on your computer and the upload/download speeds from the Internet Service Provider (ISP).

Ethernet cables are at the heart of many IP-based video production systems. Ethernet cables don't usually extend beyond 328 feet (100 meters), though they come in a variety of quality types noted below.

Category	Bandwidth
Cat-5	100 Mbps
Cat-5e	1 Gbps
CAT6	10 Gbps
CAT7	10 Gbps
CAT8	25 Gbps

Most video production setups that use ethernet for video connectivity require CAT 5e cabling or greater because regular Category 5 cabling only supports up to 100 megabits per second of data transmission.

CAT 5e supports a full gigabit, or 1,000 Megabits, of data transmission. Higher end CAT cabling can offer up to 25 gigabits of data per second.

Ethernet connections are easy and convenient to use for a variety of applications. For one thing, network connected devices can provide bi-directional connectivity to send and receive communication. You can also connect all the devices on your network to the internet, opening up many possibilities for connectivity around the world. Most commonly installed networking equipment supports gigabit connectivity, but higher bandwidth networking gear is becoming more common every day. Unfortunately, if you have 10/100 networking infrastructure, you will have a hard time using it for IP-based video production. There simply isn't enough bandwidth on these older networking systems to support HD-quality video transmission.

The good news is that gigabit networking equipment has become the industry standard and there is a good chance that this is the type of technology you have already installed. A gigabit network switch with a full throughput backplane can send approximately 1,000 megabits of data to each device on your network. You should never use 100% of the available bandwidth on your network because you need to reserve "headroom" to avoid network congestion and failure. Network bandwidth headroom recommendations can vary widely but generally, most IT professionals recommend 30% to 60% depending on what the network is used for. Consult your network administrator before adding IP video traffic to your LAN. NewTek suggests NDI® traffic should not take up more than 75% of the bandwidth of any network link.

There are many different types of network switches that can support various levels of bandwidth. While gigabit is the most popular, today you can purchase a 10-gigabit ethernet switch that provides transfer speeds of 10,000 megabits per second. Access to higher bandwidth devices will become more and more common.

	NDI HB	NDI HX 3

Codec	SpeedHQ	AVC (H.264) and HEVC (H.265)
Bandwidth 1080p60	~130Mbps	~H.264 (62Mbps) H.265 (50 Mbps)
Bandwidth at 4K60	~250Mbps	~H.264 (110Mbps) H.265 (84 Mbps)
Glass-to-glass latency	Very low	Very low
Platform Integration	CPU, FPGA	CPU, GPU. FPGA
Quality	Almost lossless	No visible compression artifacts

Note: actual bandwidth usage may vary.

Knowing how important bandwidth is to any NDI project, it's nice to know that you have some options to optimize bandwidth. The chart above shows the two main types of NDI video: NDI HB and NDI|HX. NDI HB is considered the full bandwidth version of NDI which can take a 3 gigabit, fully uncompressed video signal, and compress it down to 125-200 megabits without producing noticeable digital artifacting. This type of compression is what makes IP video production possible on a gigabit network infrastructure.

In most cases, the compression effect is "unnoticeable" to the human eye and seeing the video side-by-side is a worthwhile experience. The final destination for many live video sources is a content distribution network like Facebook and YouTube. Therefore, many users already plan to compress the entire video stream with Real Time Messaging Protocol (RTMP) or Secure Reliable Transport (SRT) before it reaches viewers.

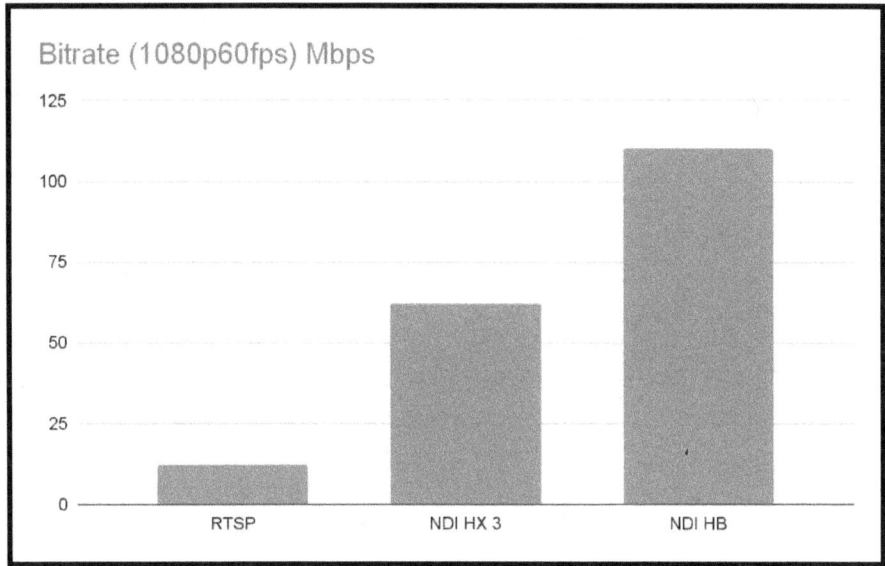

RTSP in comparison to NDI HX 3 and NDI HB.

To further advance what's possible with IP-based video production, NDI released the "High Efficiency" version of NDI called "NDI|HX." This version of NDI can compress a 1080p video source down to a mere 12-50 Mbps depending on the quality selected. NDI|HX is available in compression ratios of low, medium, high, and ultra depending on the source. All NDI sources include a "low bandwidth" option that is available in most NDI compatible software and hardware solutions.

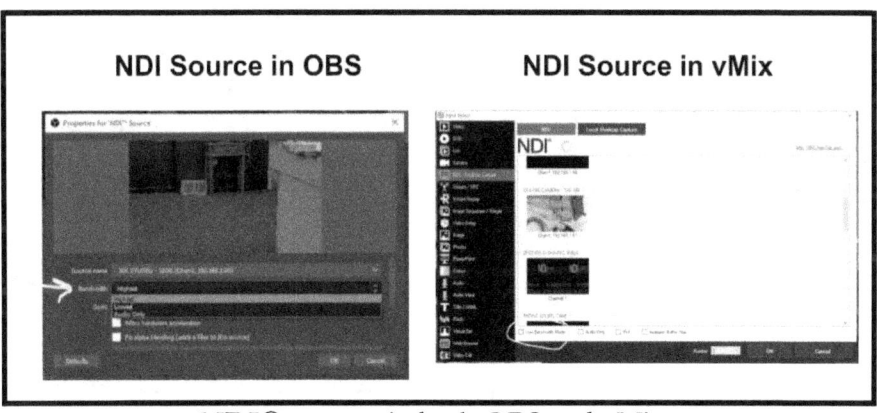

NDI® sources in both OBS and vMix.

Computers' with limited bandwidth or processing capabilities can quickly connect to NDI sources in low bandwidth mode. This is easily accomplished in most video production software solutions that support NDI. For example, when you add an NDI input in OBS, you get the option for "Highest" or "Lowest" bandwidth. Inside of vMix, you can switch to low bandwidth mode by right clicking the input. In fact, vMix allows you to discover NDI|HX sources and swap them on the fly. This is a great way for producers to conserve bandwidth and computer performance and connect to new sources on the network.

Pro Tip: Make sure to clearly name each unique NDI video source on your network. When you are reading through a list of NDI sources it is helpful to have groups of sources organized into categories. When you create NDI groups, each source will be nested inside of an organizational group which is discoverable in the network.

As you can see, there is a big difference between using NDI HB and NDI|HX sources on a network. While each NDI source will take up available bandwidth when it is used, NDI sources that are not in use will not take up any bandwidth. Therefore, you can think about NDI video sources like sockets that you can connect to at any time. When you connect to an NDI source, you are adding bandwidth through the computer's incoming Network Interface Card (NIC).

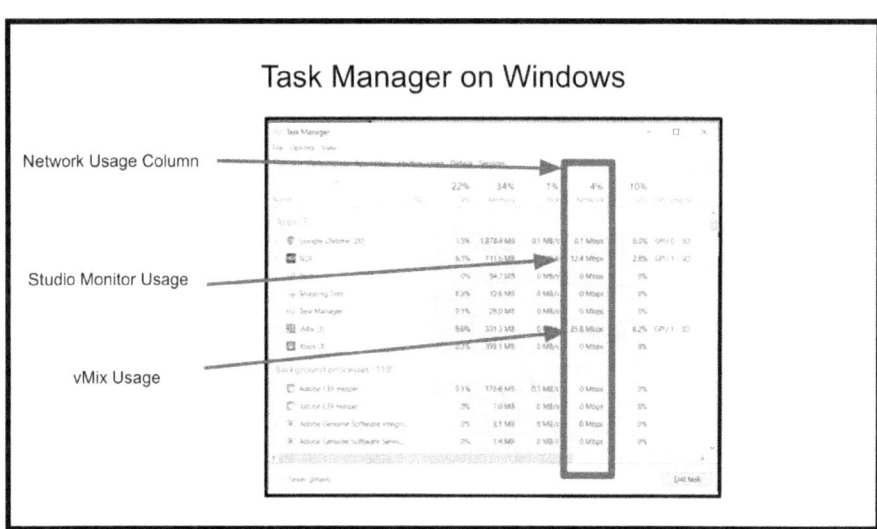

Task Manager can be used on any Windows computer to look at applications running on your computer.

Remote Production

To visualize this idea on a Windows computer, open your computer's Task Manager and look at the network utilization percentages for each process on your computer. Look at Activity Manager on a Mac computer to do the same thing. In Task Manager, there is a column that shows the network usage for the computer's NIC. There is also a "Performance" view to see bandwidth usage on a chart as shown below.

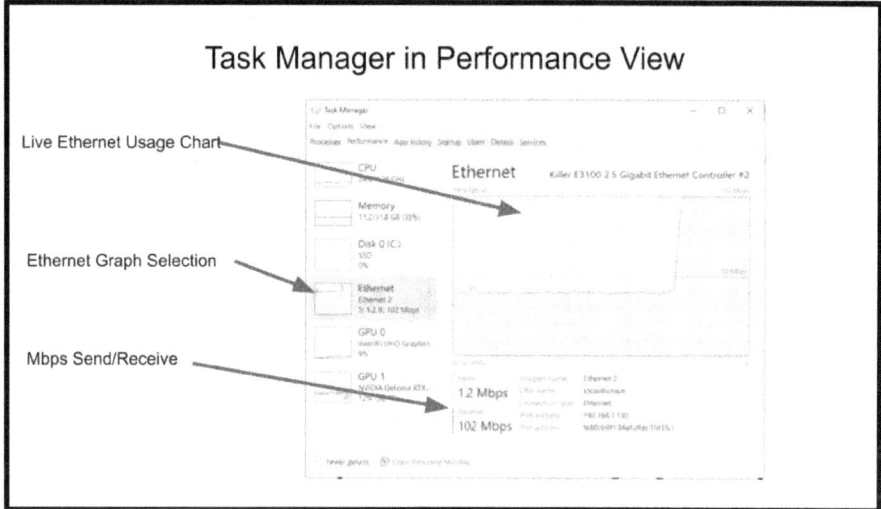

Task Manager appears in the Performance view with Ethernet selected.

The table below shows a common NDI® video use case. In this example, you will get a sense of how bandwidth accumulates in an NDI® production environment.

Example:

NDI Device Examples (1080p60fps)	Bandwidth	Accumulated Bandwidth	Total % of Gigabit Network Switch
NDI Screen Capture on Laptop for PowerPoint	125 Mbps	125 Mbps	12.5%

slides			
2 x NDI Monitors for camera operators	125 Mbps / Each	375 Mbps	12.5% / Each
vMix System output in 1080p60fps	125 Mbps	500 Mbps	12.5%
NDI Monitor in Overflow Room	125 Mbps	625 Mbps	12.5%
5 x PTZOptics NDI|HX (High)	12 Mbps / Each	685 Mbps	1.2% / Each
Suggested Headroom	250 Mbps	910 Mbps	25%
Total Usage			**91%**

As you can see, the bandwidth required for IP video projects easily adds up. Because networking equipment is so much more affordable than traditional switching hardware, many NDI® users find themselves building networks for video production.

This situation underscores the importance of understanding network backplanes. A network backplane refers to the internal data-handling capacity of a network switch, which is crucial for managing the total volume of traffic generated by all connected devices. When multiple high-bandwidth devices, such as NDI cameras and monitors, are in use, a switch with a higher backplane capacity, like 10G (Gigabits), can handle the aggregated data flow without causing bottlenecks or performance issues, especially as you get closer to the network switch bandwidth limit.

The bandwidth usage for devices like NDI cameras and monitors can quickly saturate a network. To prevent this, it's essential to factor in not just the internal traffic but also any external connections, such as internet access for systems like vMix. By doing so, network designers can ensure that the overall network remains robust, reliable, and capable of supporting both current and future demands.

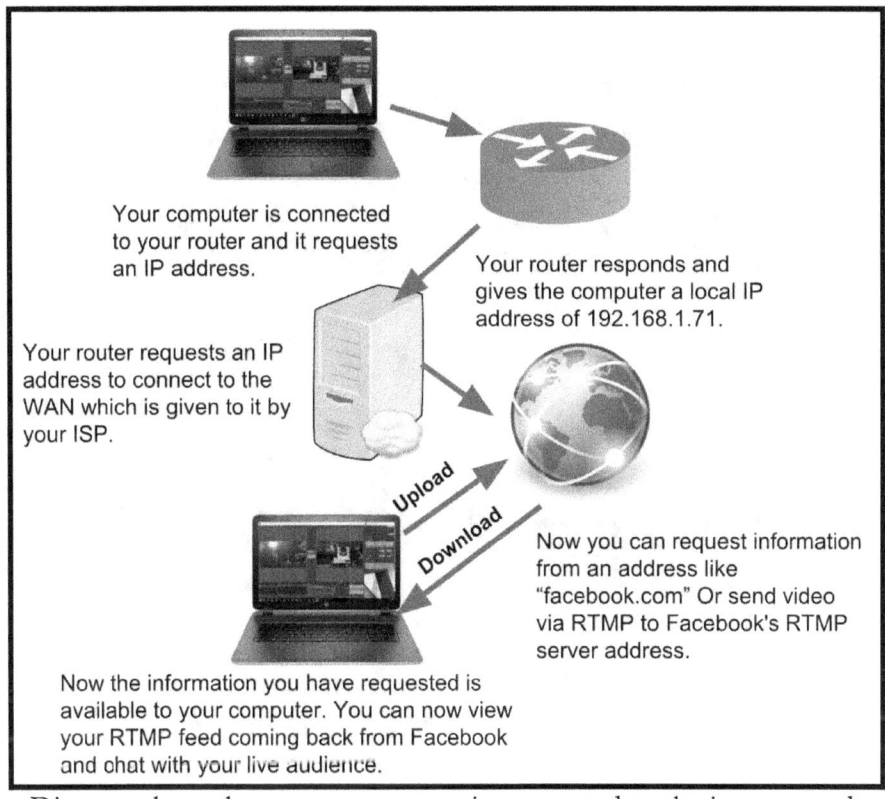

Diagram shows how your computer is connected to the internet and live streams to Facebook.

The diagram above shows how your computer is connected to your local area network. Each device connected to the LAN can request and receive information from the internet through your router. Until NDI® 5.0, almost all NDI® video traffic happened inside of the LAN. Today, NDI® Bridge and NDI® Connect allow you to securely connect with video sources outside of your LAN.

In order to live stream from inside a LAN, computers use upload bandwidth to stream video to a Content Delivery Network (CDN) such as Facebook. Once the live stream is hosted by a CDN, your computer can use download bandwidth to preview the live stream and view comments from live viewers. Video production software running on your computer like OBS or vMix can connect to multiple NDI®

sources on your LAN and then uses those sources to produce a live stream which goes out to the world using RTMP. RTMP is the primary protocol used for encoding video sent over the public internet to CDNs like YouTube.

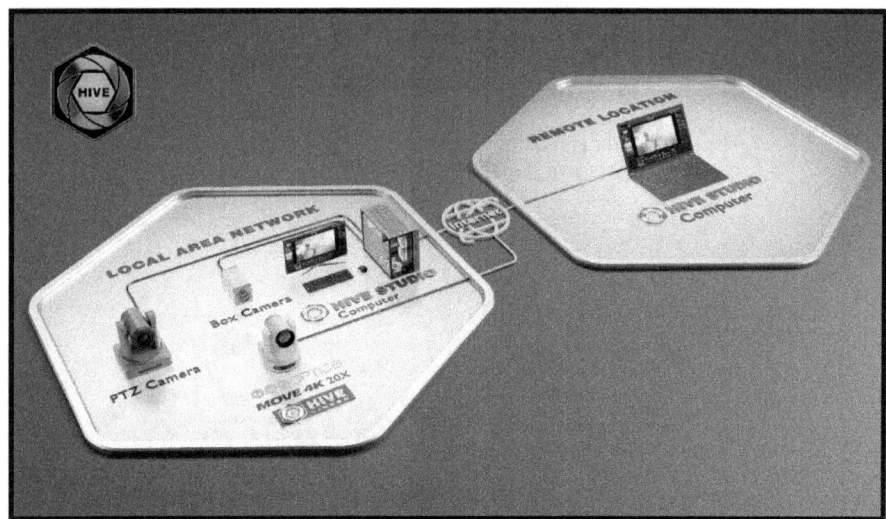

Diagram showing a studio and PTZ cameras being controlled from a remote location with Hive Studio.

Once your local area network is set up the way you want it, transitioning to the cloud can be very easy. In the diagram above, you can see that Hive Studio is set up at a remote location to control the cameras on a LAN. Two PTZ cameras are connected directly to the existing production PC and one camera is connected directly to the remote computer over the internet. Hive-Linked cameras are capable of direct connection without the need for a computer to connect the sources to the cloud.

Remote Production

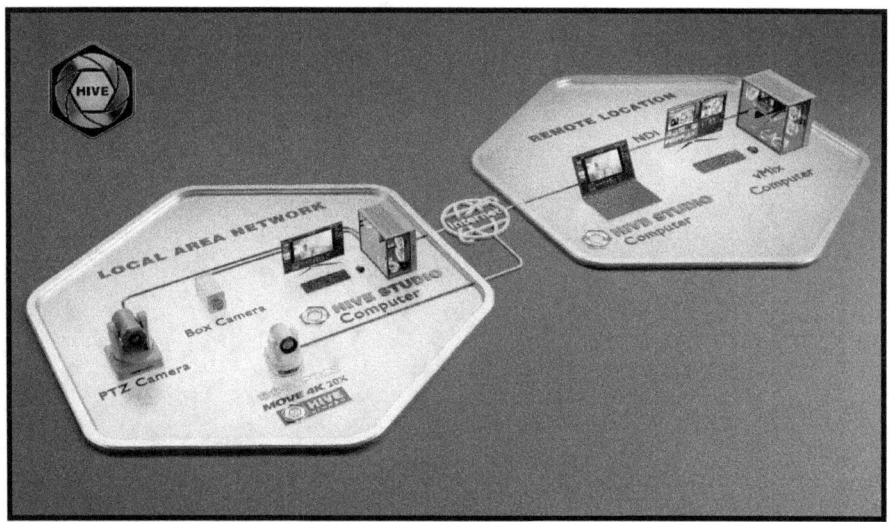

Diagram showing a studio with a remote operator connected to the system. The remote operator is controlling PTZ cameras and switching video remotely with vMix.

In this diagram, the far end is outputting NDI video to a vMix computer. In this scenario, the Hive Studio is providing remote camera control, color correction and system management, while the vMix computer is using the video sources for video switching and graphics. The vMix computer in this instance, will receive the NDI video sources from the Hive Studio computer on the remote network. Hive works as a bridge between the networks providing additional remote production features.

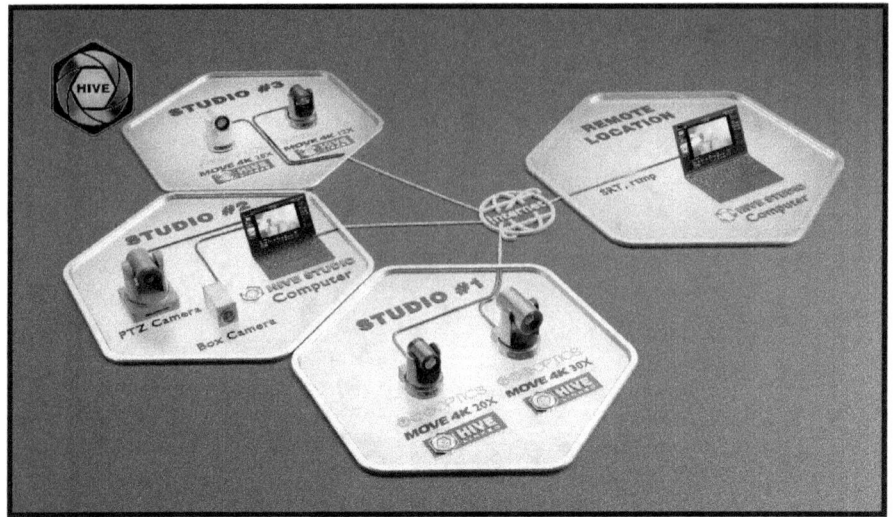

Diagram shows management of multiple studios from a remote location.

One of the nice features of the cloud is the ability to connect to multiple studios from around the world. In this diagram, a single remote computer can manage multiple studios connected through the internet. You may also have a single production studio with multiple remote operators located around the world. Remote production allows you to be creative, flexible and cost-effective as you construct new workflows that can adapt to the specific needs of your project.

KEY TAKEAWAYS FROM THIS CHAPTER:

1. **Bandwidth Limitations**: The primary bottleneck in IP video production is bandwidth limitation, which can arise from both the network infrastructure and the Internet Service Provider (ISP). Understanding the bandwidth requirements of your production and ensuring sufficient flexibility is crucial.

2. **NDI Technology**: NDI HB (High Bandwidth): Supports compression of a fully uncompressed 3-gigabit video signal to 125-200 megabits, facilitating HD video production on gigabit networks. NDI|HX (High Efficiency): Allows further compression of 1080p video down to 8-50 Mbps, suitable for

varying quality needs and available in multiple compression ratios.

3. **Monitoring Network Usage**: Tools like Windows Task Manager and macOS Activity Monitor can be used to monitor network utilization, helping manage and optimize network performance for video production.

4. **Live Streaming Setup**: Video production software like OBS or vMix can connect to NDI sources within a LAN and use RTMP to stream video to CDNs like YouTube and Facebook, leveraging both upload and download bandwidth effectively.

5. **Cloud Integration**: Cloud-based systems allow connecting multiple studios globally, enhancing the capability to manage and operate remote productions across different locations. This supports a flexible, creative, and cost-effective approach to constructing new workflows tailored to specific project needs.

11 THE NDI BRIDGE, SRT & VMIX IN THE CLOUD

NDI Bridge is a tool designed for sharing NDI video sources beyond a local area network (LAN) using the Wide Area Network (WAN), also known as the "Public Internet." NDI Bridge was released in 2021 with the NDI 5.0 toolset, along with NDI Remote and Audio Direct tools. Until NDI Bridge was released, many video productions used NDI only for LAN video traffic and relied on technologies such as Secure Reliable Transport (SRT) or video communication solutions like Zoom to transport video over the public internet. NDI 5.0 supports a technology called Reliable User Datagram Protocol (RUDP) which is a point-to-point video transport protocol that allows for high quality video transport over public networks.

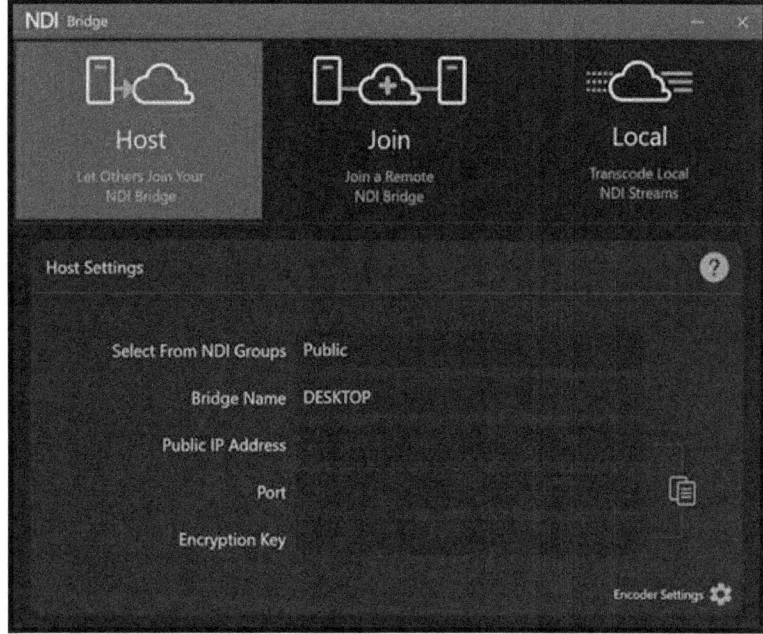

NDI Bridge application open to the "Host" tab.

The NDI Bridge has three main components that allow users to advertise and transport NDI video over the WAN. First, users can set up their Host connection. The Host connection allows others to join the NDI Bridge that is set-up on one side of the connection. Here, you can select a group of NDI sources to be transported over the WAN to a receiving location anywhere in the world. You will learn more about setting up groups of NDI sources with Access Manager in the next chapter. Using NDI Groups, the NDI Bridge can send an entire group of NDI HB or NDI HX video sources together over the public internet.

NDI Bridge does require a public IP address and an open port to operate properly. You can request a public IP address through your Internet Service Provider (ISP). Or, you can use a dynamic DNS provider like No-IP to use a hostname instead. Ports for video traffic can be created through the router connected to the WAN. Once the public IP address and open port are set up, a host connection can be accessed through the public internet.

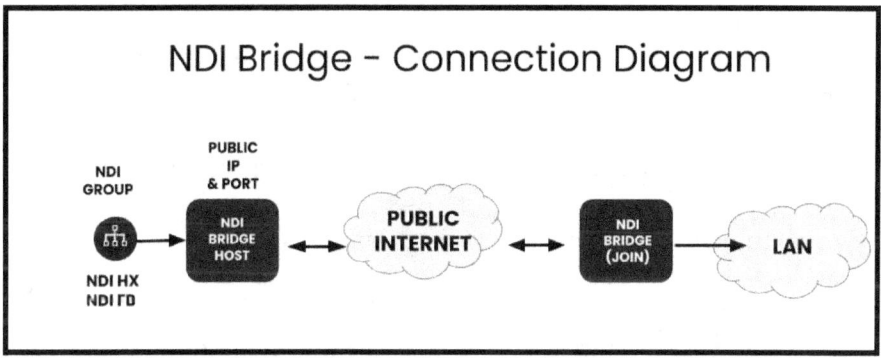

NDI Bridge connection diagram uses the public internet.

From the far end of an NDI Bridge connection, the same outside IP address and port number information is necessary to send video. Once both ends of the NDI Bridge are connected, the NDI sources available on the host side will be made available for the far end side to use just like local NDI sources.

NDI Bridge supports NDI video source capabilities including alpha channel, PTZ controls, KVM, Tally, and Metadata. Alpha channel support is necessary for many broadcast graphics applications. Graphics overlays are a use case for NDI Bridge used with alpha channel video. Alpha channel video supports a transparent background that overlays on top of another video source. In this way, NDI Bridge allows remote productions to bring alpha channel graphics into a production environment from anywhere in the world.

PTZ camera controls open up another interesting use case in which NDI Bridge is used to send video from a PTZ camera where the PTZ cameras can be controlled from a remote location. KVM, a popular abbreviation for "Keyboard, Video, and Mouse" can be used to pass along remote controls for computer screens captured with KVM support.

NDI Bridge will also maintain support for Tally, the technology that alerts camera operators and on-screen talent when a camera is in use. This is an interesting feature which would allow a remote production to know when a specific NDI video source is being used even from a remote production. The Tally feature of NDI will be discussed in more detail in Chapter 19. Finally, some metadata is also transported over the NDI Bridge which includes information such as NDI source-friendly names. Metadata makes NDI video more usable by providing information that compatible NDI systems can use to display relevant information to producers working with the video.

While NDI Bridge does have some technical requirements before it can work, it provides powerful connectivity options. In comparison to established wide area network (WAN) video transport solutions like Secure Reliable Transport (SRT), NDI simplifies set-up by requiring a single port to support multiple video channels. NDI Bridge provides the opportunity for many productions to think outside of their own local area networks (LAN) to implement video projects that incorporate video from around the world.

NDI Bridge in Virtual Environments

Using NDI Bridge in a Virtual Machine (VM) offers a host of benefits for producing high-quality live events, particularly in optimizing resource efficiency, enhancing flexibility, improving performance, providing redundancy, and ensuring both security and ease of maintenance. By running NDI Bridge in a VM, precise allocation of necessary resources is enabled, freeing up additional resources for other tasks and optimizing overall hardware utilization.

VMs significantly enhance the flexibility of managing software configurations. They facilitate easy switching between setups and simplify the process of creating backups and replicating systems—key advantages in dynamic production environments. When VMs support Graphics Processing Unit (GPU) passthrough, this feature can dramatically improve the performance of NDI Bridge by harnessing the GPU's capabilities for intensive video processing tasks such as encoding and decoding, which are crucial for real-time streaming.

Furthermore, operating NDI Bridge within a VM environment enables the maintenance of multiple instances, providing critical redundancy and ensuring backup instances are ready to deploy in case of system failure, thus enhancing the reliability of live productions. VMs also bolster the overall stability and security of the operating environment; by isolating NDI Bridge within a VM, any potential crashes or errors are confined to the VM itself, minimizing the risk to the entire system. Security issues within the VM are similarly contained.

In terms of maintenance, VMs make it easier to isolate problems and perform system troubleshooting. Should issues arise with NDI Bridge, the system can be quickly restored to a previous state, or a new VM can be set up without affecting the main operating system.

However, it's important to acknowledge the potential drawbacks. Running NDI Bridge in a VM introduces additional complexity and overhead, and setting up GPU passthrough might be challenging depending on the specific hardware and software environment. These factors should be carefully weighed against the needs and constraints of the specific production environment to determine if using NDI Bridge in a VM is the most suitable approach.

Understanding SRT

SRT is a video transport protocol designed to send high quality video over the public internet. SRT stands for Secure, Reliable, Transport. SRT can be used with many popular video production solutions including OBS, Wirecast, and vMix. In fact, there are over 450 members in the SRT alliance. SRT is used by video producers small and large to enable remote productions from all around the world.

Unlike NDI, which is designed for local area networks, SRT was designed for use over the public internet. This is done partially by managing a fixed amount of latency for each video stream. SRT video connections provide broadcast studios remote access to high definition video and audio that is usable for video production. For example, SRT is an ideal way to send video from reporters in the field who make remote video contributions. Broadcast studios can then receive that video in a way that it can be mixed into a news production.

SRT has made a name for itself by providing encryption that ensures secure transport of even the highest level production. SRT can enable end-to-end AES encryption which is ideal for any content that requires protection. SRT protects against video jitter and packet loss even during bandwidth fluctuations from unreliable WiFi or cellular connections.

As SRT hardware and software has become more affordable, everyday productions done at schools, churches and state/local government agencies are using the solution. While SRT is used by the world's largest live production companies including Fox Sports, Comcast, and the NFL, the solution is open source and used by thousands of independent broadcasters.

SRT is helping to enable remote productions around the world, and there are a few things you should know to get started using SRT.

First of all, SRT uses the public internet. Therefore, you can either set up a peer-to-peer connection or you can use a proxy server to connect. A peer-to-peer connection will require a little networking knowledge. For example, you will need to know your public IP address (or dynamic DNS hostname), make sure your router is set up with port forwarding, and configure your video production software to receive the stream. There are great tutorials you can watch to step through this process, like this one on vMix's YouTube channel. The second easier way to get set up using SRT is to use a SRTMiniServer in combination with its proxy server capabilities. This application which costs $30 per month, will receive SRT video feeds and convert them into NDI which you can easily use with OBS, vMix, Wirecast and more.

You should know that SRT is not ideal for two-way communications like Zoom or Skype. Rather, SRT is ideal for broadcasting in one-way communication scenarios like remote reporting and connecting video streams to a remote broadcast studio. One of our favorite use cases for SRT is remote production with a couple of 5G connected cell phones. The Urbanist recently produced a multi-camera tour of NYC using the Lorax Broadcaster App on iPhone 12 cameras. These cameras were able to send 2-3 Mbps quality video streams back to a production PC which was then incorporated broadcast elements such as live chat, graphics, overlays and more.

REMOTE PRODUCTION
PRO TIP

vMix does a great job explaining SRT with both Caller and Listener modes in this video.

Another great example of SRT, is connecting two video production systems together. For example, consider a trade show happening where a live stream is going on. A company can easily set up a few cameras on site, but they don't need to bring an entire video production system with them on site. Instead, they can send each video and audio stream from the tradeshow floor back to their video production studio for broadcasting out to the world.

Note: When using the hardware encoding option in a software like vMix you can utilize an NVIDIA graphics card to decode SRT video streams. When doing so, you may need to consider how many encoding channels are being utilized on your graphics card for use simultaneously. If your graphics card has a limited number of simultaneous encoding channels you may need to use your CPU to decode SRT. Most Geforce NVIDIA graphics cards are limited to two hardware encodes per system. So if you are using hardware encoding for your recording and streaming you cannot also not use it for SRT with a Geforce graphics card. If you have a P2000 or higher end Quadro Card you can have an unlimited number of encodes. Quadro graphics cards are only limited by the capabilities of the particular card.

SRT & vMix in the Cloud

SRT has become a preferred method of video transport when sending video to a cloud production server. vMix supports SRT ingestion and the software is particularly good with pulling SRT video together for remote production. vMix supports SRT video as both an input and an output, allowing for flexibility in many complex productions. You can also use SRT video inputs with the vMix MultiCorder allowing you to record each incoming SRT stream independently for post-production.

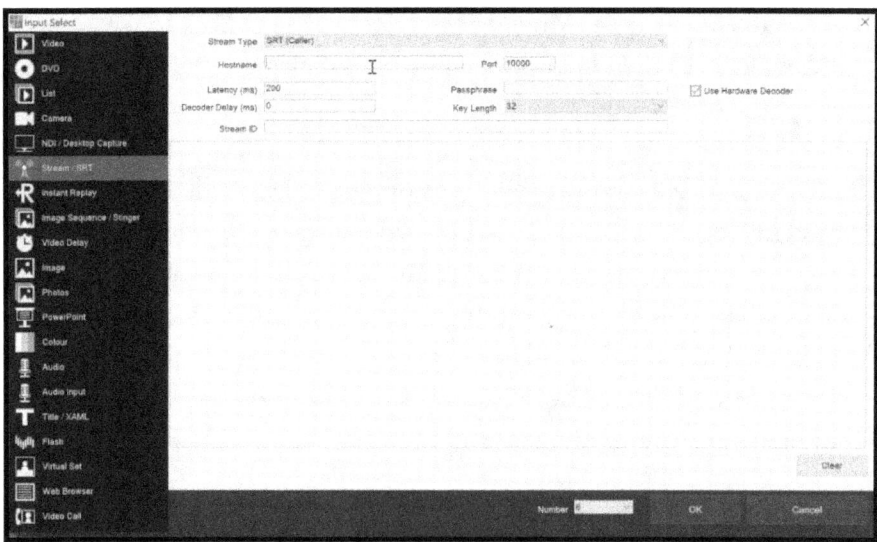

SRT Input Select in vMix, allows you to bring SRT video sources into vMix for video switching and recording.

Running vMix in the cloud involves setting up a Windows server instance with specific requirements, including a directly attached graphics card with virtual display support, typically provided under technologies like NVIDIA Grid. This setup ensures that vMix can leverage the powerful graphics processing capabilities needed for high-quality live video production. Cloud deployment of vMix is ideal for users needing flexible, high-performance broadcasting capabilities without the physical constraints of traditional hardware setups. However, it's crucial to test the cloud setup thoroughly to ensure it meets the demands of live production, especially since performance can vary due to the shared nature of cloud services.

You can learn more about running Vmix in the cloud in Chapter 10, Advanced Topics in Remote Production.

KEY TAKEAWAYS FROM THIS CHAPTER:

1. **NDI Bridge Enhances Remote Production**: Released as part of the NDI 5.0 toolset in 2021, NDI Bridge allows the extension of NDI video sources beyond a local area network using the public internet. This technology uses Reliable User Datagram Protocol (RUDP) to facilitate high-quality video transport over wide area networks (WAN), effectively connecting distant production sites.

2. **Technical Setup for NDI Bridge**: For effective use, NDI Bridge requires a public IP address or dynamic DNS hostname and an open port, allowing video traffic through the internet. Users can set up a host connection, select NDI sources to be shared over the WAN, and establish secure and efficient video source transportation to any global location.

3. **Advanced Features Supported by NDI Bridge**: NDI Bridge supports comprehensive video production capabilities including alpha channel for broadcast graphics, PTZ camera controls, KVM for remote screen control, Tally for on-air source

indication, and metadata transport. These features enable a broad range of remote production scenarios.

4. **Utilization in Virtual Environments**: NDI Bridge can be operated within a virtual machine (VM) to enhance resource efficiency, flexibility, performance, security, and ease of maintenance. VMs allow for precise resource allocation and simplify the process of system backup and recovery, making NDI Bridge more robust in dynamic production environments.

5. **SRT and vMix Integration for Cloud-Based Production**: Secure Reliable Transport (SRT) has become a preferred method for transmitting video to cloud production servers, with vMix offering robust support for SRT ingestion. This integration allows vMix to handle SRT video both as an input and output, adding substantial flexibility to complex productions. Additionally, vMix can run in a cloud environment on a Windows server with a high-performance graphics card, making it a versatile option for remote broadcasting where physical hardware limitations are a constraint. This setup is particularly effective for productions that require high-quality live video processing capabilities, though it is essential to thoroughly test the cloud deployment to ensure optimal performance during live productions.

12 Remote Production Workflows and Team Roles

In the fast-paced world of remote broadcasting, efficiency in operations is not merely an advantage—it's a necessity. It's important to create the workflow that aligns with the skills and tools specific to your team's roles. This alignment leads to quicker turnaround times and more effective resource utilization, crucial in high-pressure environments where precision and speed are vital.

For producers, the workflow should enable coordination across the production team. Camera operators benefit from workflows that allow for seamless integration with remote technologies such as robotic PTZ cameras. Color correction specialists require workflows that support high-fidelity color grading tools to maintain visual coherence throughout the footage. Audio mixers thrive in environments where audio feeds are effortlessly integrated and remotely manageable.

Scalability is another vital consideration, particularly in response to fluctuating audience sizes and market demands. A scalable workflow accommodates growth or contraction without extensive overhauls—essential for maintaining continuous operations and cost-effectiveness. This is especially important in remote production settings, where adapting quickly to new technologies and processes can significantly impact performance and output quality.

Understanding the diverse roles within a remote production team is crucial for optimizing workflow and enhancing the overall quality of the production. The following table breaks down key positions, highlighting their responsibilities, required skills, tools and equipment used, and the outcomes they are expected to deliver. This structure helps in identifying how each role contributes to the success of the production, ensuring that all team members are equipped with the necessary resources and skills to perform their tasks effectively. Whether overseeing the project as a producer, capturing visuals as a camera operator, fine-tuning the aesthetics as a color correction specialist, or balancing the audio landscape as an audio mixer, each role is vital to delivering a polished final product.

Role	Responsibilities	Skills Required	Tools/Equipment Used	Key Outputs
Producer	Oversees the entire production process, manage the budget, coordinates among different departments, ensures timeline adherence	Leadership, budget management, comms, problem-solving	Production software like ShoFlo, communication tools	Completed production, managed team, budget reports
Director	Calls the shots, selecting among many different sources to tell a cohesive story	Visual story-telling, live, real-time show management, switcher operations, calm, cool demeanor in stressful situations	Hardware & software production switchers, production software, communication tools	Program Output for live streaming and/or "live-to-tape" recording
Technical Director (TD)	Control the production switcher and other control room technologies		All control-room-based technologies	Program and other outputs for live streaming & recording

Role	Responsibilities	Skills	Equipment	Outcome
Camera Operator	Operates cameras during live events, ensure proper framing, focusing and movement	Camera handling, technical knowledge of broadcast cameras, attention to detail	Cameras, tripods, monitors	High-quality video footage
Color Correction Specialist	Adjusts color settings to ensure video quality consistency across various shots	Color theory, video editing software proficiency, attention to detail	Camera Control Units (CCUs) video editing software, calibrated monitors	Matched cameras, Visually coherent footage
Audio Mixer	Manages and adjust audio feed during production, mix sound sources, ensure clear audio output	Audio mixing, knowledge of sound equipment, acute hearing	Audio mixing console, microphones, headphones	High-quality audio feed
Graphics Specialist	Manages all the static and animated graphics for production	Some basic graphic design, text layout, live event experience, attention to detail	Photoshop, PowerPoint, New Blue FX, Singular.Live, etc.	

Description of Each Role

1. **Producer**: The producer is akin to a project manager and is

responsible for the overall execution of the production. This client-facing role involves high-level planning, budgeting, and coordination among all other roles to ensure the production runs smoothly and meets its objectives.

2. **Director:** The director is responsible for "telling the story" of the show by calling the camera shots and other sources that can be mixed together in the video switcher. Sometimes this role is combined with the producer role and/or the technical director role. Whether working in a combined role (common on smaller, less complex projects) or discrete roles, the person in this role is responsible for guiding the efforts of all production crew members. In the live events world, this role is sometimes called "show caller" and includes directing the activities of Zoom/Teams specialists who manage remote participants, open/close breakout rooms and who launch polls and surveys.

3. **Technical Director:** Like the name suggests, the technical director (TD) is responsible for the set-up and operations of the control room technology. This person may be a "one-man-band" who, in addition to operating the live production switcher, controls shading (camera coloring), video playback, graphics, sound, encoding, recording and all other aspects of control room production. When in a more discrete role, the technical director takes his cues from the director. Often the director and TD are the same person—especially in smaller, less complex and budget-constrained productions.

4. **Camera Operator:** This role focuses on the technical aspects of filming. The camera operator is responsible for capturing the live action as per the director's vision. This includes making real-time decisions about shot selection, camera movement, and focus.

5. **Color Correction Specialist:** After footage is captured, the

color correction specialist ensures that the footage maintains consistent quality and color accuracy. This role is critical for post-production, enhancing the visual appeal and ensuring that the footage has a uniform look.

6. **Audio Mixer:** Responsible for all aspects of sound during a production, the audio mixer manages live audio mixing and ensures that the audio quality is maintained at a high standard. This role is crucial for live broadcasts where audio cues and ambient sound need to be balanced with dialogue.

7. **Graphics Specialist:** often called a graphics operator, the person in this role takes their cues from the director to ensure that the right text, PowerPoint, photos, images and animations are fed into the production switcher (and started/advanced) at the right time.

Remote Production Workflow: Producer

A producer's job starts long before the event begins. This can involve project management in general which involves a high level understanding of the entire workflow. Producers may even manage equipment and use an equipment management system such as Cheqroom or CurrentRMS. From understanding the gear necessary to complete a project, to tracking gear availability and scheduling a producer's job is never easy.

Producers often create proposals for clients and have a strong understanding of client expectations. Even when sales and project management roles are separated from the producer's task, they are often responsible for the end product, down to the details of when to cut between which source.

A pro tip for new producers, 95% of camera transitions are the CUT function. New producers often overuse fancy transitions such as stingers, merges and crossfades. While they look great, they can actually be distracting if overused. With that being said, stinger transitions can be effectively used when transitioning from live camera feeds to other types of media such as instant-replay footage or a presentation.

Remote Production Workflow: Camera Operator

In remote production workflows, the camera operator plays a crucial role that blends technical knowledge with artistic vision. Camera operators need to be adept at managing their equipment, understanding key functions like zoom and focus controls, white balance, and shutter speed. Technical proficiency is essential because operators must ensure all camera settings are optimized for each shot and be able to troubleshoot issues promptly. This is crucial to maintain seamless production, even when working remotely where on-site support may be limited.

Next, the operator must apply these technical skills practically by mastering shot composition. They should be well-versed in principles like the rule of thirds, headroom, and lead room to frame subjects effectively, creating visually engaging shots. They also need to adjust their camera movement based on the producer/director's vision, ensuring smooth transitions and dynamic angles that align with the production's overall style.

The artistic component is equally vital in this role. While it's challenging to formally teach artistic vision, camera operators must be encouraged to observe how professionals craft compelling visuals, to experiment creatively, and to listen and anticipate changes in the production environment. In remote setups, this means staying highly attuned to the director's guidance and reacting swiftly to evolving demands.

Robotic PTZ cameras have traditionally been difficult to remotely control. In fact, I wrote a book called the *PTZ Camera Operators Handbook* in 2022, which may serve as a helpful reference for those new to PTZ camera operation. Many advancements have been made over the past couple of years including auto-tracking and auto-framing. Auto-tracking allows PTZ cameras to automatically lock in on a specific subject and track that person with pan, tilt and zoom movements. Auto-framing is a similar technology designed to maintain specific framing (i.e. MCU, MS, WS with specific headroom or left/right lead room) while panning, tilting and zooming to follow a single subject or a group. Auto-framing can also imply that all subjects in view will be framed using automated pan, tilt and zoom movements.

PTZOptics Hive PTZ camera movement tools. Click to Center is highlighted.

In addition to automation tools, more powerful manual robotic camera tools have been developed as well. The image above shows several of the PTZOptics Hive robotic camera tools that allow remote operators more control over their cameras. Click to Center is a simple yet powerful way to quickly move PTZ cameras to the correct location during a broadcast. Hive also offers a "Cine-Center" option for moving the camera more slowly and gracefully when it is being done during a live broadcast. The next tool in the image above, is called "Fast-Frame" which is used to choose any size frame on screen and have the PTZ camera move directly to that location. These tools represent the next generation of PTZ camera movement tools, as they enable productivity gains for camera operators.

In summary, the remote production camera operator must seamlessly merge technical skills with creative intuition, adapting fluidly to dynamic conditions while delivering high-quality visuals that enrich the production. Their work contributes significantly to the overall storytelling, as their shots bring the narrative to life even from afar.

Remote Production Workflow: Color Correction

For remote color correction, you can effectively employ two distinct approaches—adjusting the camera settings directly and using live production software. Below is a structured table that outlines each method, highlighting their benefits and considerations:

Approach	Description	Key Settings/Tools	Benefits
Camera Settings Adjustment	This method involves directly configuring camera settings such as Iris, Shutter Speed, Gain, and built-in Color Correction to achieve the desired image quality at the source	Iris, Shutter Speed, Gain, Color Correction	Optimizes image quality from the start, adhering to the principle of "garbage in, garbage out," where the quality of input directly influences the output. Ensures the best raw ISO (isolated individual camera) recorded footage for post-production
Color Correction in Live Software	Utilizes software tools within live production environments to adjust colors and correct images during the production process	Live production software, color grading tools such as Vectorscope and Waveform Monitor	Allows for flexible, real-time adjustments and enhancements during live events, providing the ability to adapt to changing lighting conditions and other variables on the fly ISO recordings DO NOT include color correction

1. **Camera Settings Adjustment**: This approach is foundational, as it ensures that the footage captured is of the highest possible quality right from the camera. Adjusting settings like Iris and Shutter Speed helps in controlling the exposure, while Gain and Color Correction settings adjust the brightness and color balance, respectively. This proactive method minimizes the need for extensive post-production correction, aligning with the concept that the quality of output is only as good as the quality of input. Ensuring high-quality input is critical in remote production, where real-time corrections might be limited.

2. **Color Correction in Live Software**: When using live production software, the color correction process becomes part of the live editing workflow. This method is highly adaptable, allowing operators to make immediate adjustments based on the live feed. It is particularly useful in dynamic environments where lighting conditions can change throughout the day or unexpectedly (like when a presenter walks out into an unlit audience) or when multiple cameras with slightly different color profiles are used.

Both approaches have their distinct advantages and can be used in conjunction depending on the production's specific needs and the environment. The choice of method often depends on the level of control required and the nature of the broadcast event.

Remotely controlling color correction is a great workflow utilized by professionals who need multiple cameras color corrected for a live event. vMix is an excellent tool for this purpose, featuring robust camera color correction tools such as a vectorscope and waveform monitor. In this workflow, we will demonstrate the use of several PTZOptics Hive-linked cameras, which are capable of sending NDI video feeds to a Local Area Network (LAN) from a remote location by leveraging the cloud connection to Hive. Once the NDI video sources are accessible on the LAN, we can proceed to color correct them using vMix.

Colour Correction Tools

Waveform Monitor	Vectorscope	Waveform + Vectorscope + Preview

A big part of making your live production look great is making sure your colors look realistic and match from camera to camera. vMix includes color correction tools that are advanced enough for color optimization experts yet simple enough that average users, especially those with video editing experience can improve their productions' overall look. Color correction tools are available on every video input, including cameras, videos, and images.

To start, set all cameras to the same color temperature. If possible, place all cameras next to each other and have them shoot the same subject at the same time — such as a wide shot of a scene. In the past, video engineers would place a black and white logarithmic reflectance chart called a "chip chart" on a music stand for all cameras to shoot, but today's easy-to-use color controls don't require that — though almost any modern color chart can serve as a good starting point.. The basic idea is to first adjust flesh tones, then the other colors and black, white and gray values look natural and creatively satisfactory—on one camera (your "reference" camera) and then share those settings with other cameras and tweak them (one at a time) until you don't notice any changes in the color, black, white or gray images among cameras. This is a "best outcome" and will sometimes require some time and patience to achieve - or at least come very close. Using a vectorscope & waveform monitor, as described below, can help.

Color Correction Tools

For exacting color control, select **Colour Correction** from the input settings menu to access the professional color correction tools. The interface offers control over the lift, gamma, and gain. The lift adjusts the dark areas of the image, the gamma impacts the gray values in between black and white, and the gain adjusts the bright areas of the image.

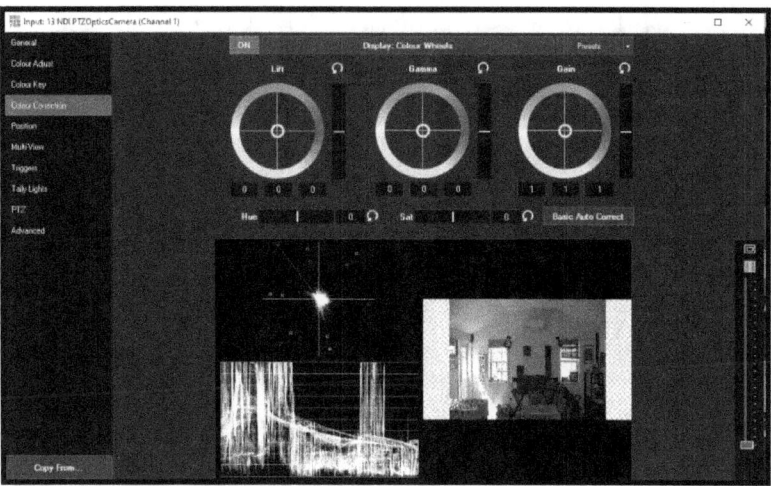

The most basic function on this menu is the Basic Auto Correct button that attempts to set the lift and gain controls to their optimum setting. Also found on this page are several reset buttons shaped as a circular arrow to undo any settings that you would like reverted to default. The "copy from" at the bottom left-hand corner of this window allows you to copy the color settings from any other input—which is useful as a starting point, especially when using multiples of the same camera.

Color Wheels

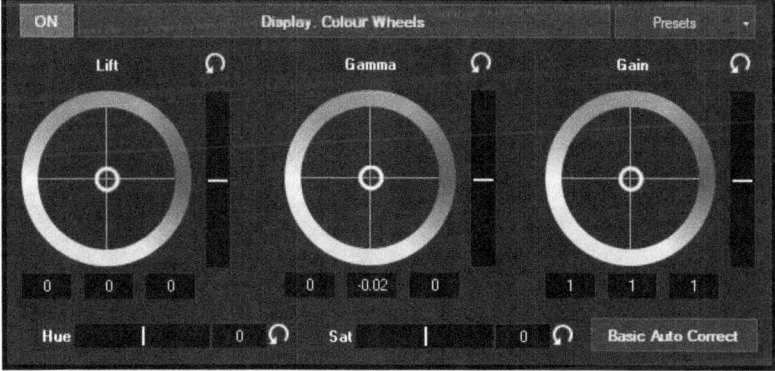

The color correction tools inside vMix have three (3) wheels which are used commonly in video editing software. The first wheel represents the blacks (shadows) also called lift. The second wheel represents gamma or mid tones and the third wheel represents the highlights and overall brightness of the image. Each wheel adjusts a particular part of the image. The first wheel can be used to work with dark areas, the middle wheel works on areas which are usually skin tones and the final wheel is for the highlights. Using the three components of the color correction wheels allows operators the ability to do fine color correction in an intuitive layout. You can use gain control, for example, to adjust the yellows just in the highlight of an image.

Adjustment can be made on the color wheel by dragging the circle to the desired location. Adjustments can be made to all colors equally by using the Luminance/Brightness bar to the wheel's right. Hue and saturation can be adjusted using the bar below the wheels.

Pro Tip: Try using the ON/OFF buttons to see the color corrections you have applied. Sometimes it's worth seeing all of the changes you have made by looking back at the original.

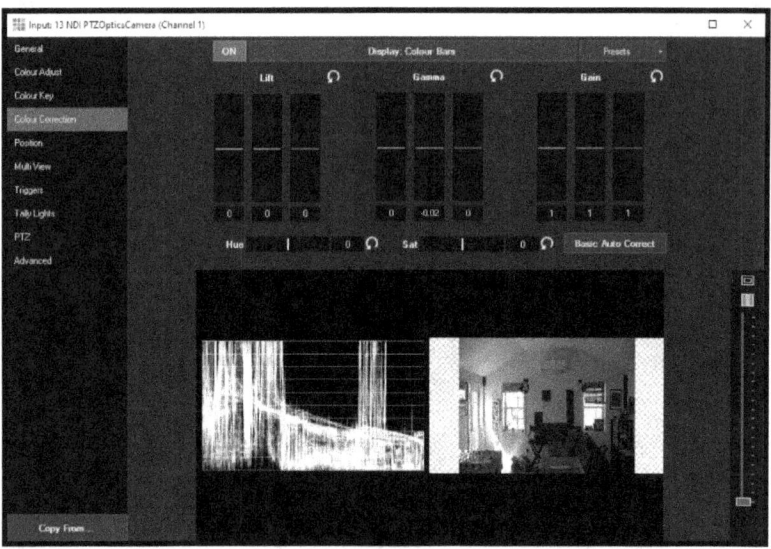

Color Bars

By clicking on **Display Color Bars** at the top, the view will be changed to color bars here. The red, green, and blue levels can be adjusted independently for lift, gamma, and gain. Color bars are easier to operate than wheels because wheels are constantly adjusting multiple colors with every change. Bars allow you to adjust a single color independent of others. If you are just learning how to perform color corrections or you are trying to fix a specific color issue, color bars may be easier for you to operate than wheels.

What is a Vectorscope?

A Vectorscope is a tool that represents the colors within your image. It's a graphic representation of the individual colors and the amount (chromanance/saturation) of each for the input currently in Vmix's preview window. The various boxes represent the colors in NTSC color bars and their relationship to each other—red, magenta, blue cyan, green and yellow. Caucasian flesh tone usually appears on the diagonal line between red and yellow. A Vectorscope is a tool that is ideal for live video color correction without having to rely on your own eyes and potentially inaccurate monitor representations of an image. The key is to look for little to no variation when switching among cameras in preview—making minute adjustments to all but your reference camera.

What is a Waveform Monitor?

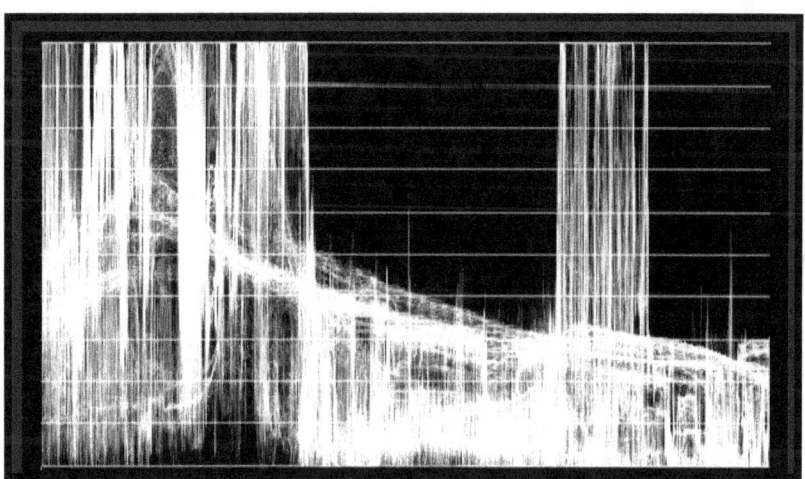

For those with color correction experience or those who want to learn, vMix also includes several types of Waveform Monitors. The Waveform Monitor is the counterpart to the Vectorscope and measures white, black and gray levels relating to brightness, contrast and exposure. With a Waveform Monitor, you can easily see if the whites in your image are clipping (flat line) at the top or if the blacks (at the bottom) are being crushed (often purposefully). You can also see the gray values change when you adjust gamma. The Waveform Monitor will allow camera operators the ability to adjust the image preferably in the camera first to ensure your image has a good exposure.

Ideally, you want your camera's image to be within the limits of your Waveform Monitor. You can use vMix to make sure your video has appropriate whites and blacks using the tools as needed. Flesh tone usually looks natural at 70% (which broadcasters call 70 IRE units) and whites max out at 100%, though may lose detail at that setting or higher. Blacks usually look normal at 7.5% but can sometimes be "crushed" (lowered) to increase contrast, but may lose detail too.

The tool can be accessed by clicking the small color bar box on the right side of the video preview. Each of the waveform monitor options can be viewed in a split-screen with a preview of the input or in a full screen independently. These are essential for completing precise luminance, correction adjustments—even across colors. Using the slide on the right, the zoom level of the image can be adjusted. Users can make adjustments to the color setting wheels and bars while seeing the precise impact on the waveform monitors. This can often help even novices detect and correct luminance, lift and gamma issues.

Remote Production Workflow: Audio Mixing Role

In a remote production workflow, the broadcast audio engineer is crucial for achieving high-quality sound in live broadcasts and recordings. With advancements in technology, audio engineers can now work from remote locations instead of being tied to the event venue (except for the public address (PA) mixer at the venue). This flexibility allows centralized management, reduces costs, and ensures consistent sound quality across multiple broadcasts.

The primary responsibilities of an audio mixer include overseeing microphone setup, ensuring clear signal capture, and managing sound levels from various sources. They often use digital mixing consoles, whether physical or virtual, to balance audio channels for dialogue, music, sound effects, and ambient noise. Collaboration with the production team is essential to align audio with visual and narrative elements, while technical troubleshooting skills help quickly resolve sound issues.

Modern audio mixers also integrate automation and artificial intelligence (AI) tools, like automix and noise reduction features, to simplify their tasks and maintain consistent sound quality. Familiarity with digital signal processing (DSP) systems and network protocols, such as Dante or AES67, is helpful in managing signal routing and processing.

In summary, the audio mixing role in a remote production workflow is all about maintaining cohesive, high-quality sound that aligns with the artistic vision of the production. With new technology making it easier to work remotely, the role continues to evolve to meet the growing demands of modern broadcasting.

Team Communications

Remote productions require a seamless flow of communication to synchronize activities across various locations. Effective use of communication tools like Discord, Unity, or Zoom is critical to maintaining a cohesive team dynamic and ensuring that project milestones are met. These tools not only facilitate straightforward communication but also support complex collaborative needs involving multimedia sharing and real-time feedback. At the 2024 NAB live stream I mentioned earlier in this book we used Unity Intercom to communicate with the remote production team in Florida. Unity is a smartphone and computer-based based intercom system. If you are managing a remote team that is involved in live production, communication is key. Learning how to utilize these communication systems effectively determines the efficiency and success of remote productions.

Here are three prominent communication platforms: Discord, Unity

Intercom and Zoom (or any conferencing app). Well known broadcast intercom maker Clearcom uses a hybrid approach that allows their wired and wireless intercom systems to connect to their web-based servers and then to cell phones running their Agent IC app.

REMOTE PRODUCTION PRO TIP

You can create your own Discord server for free and use it for team communication. Try it today.

Discord

Discord, originally popularized among gaming communities, has evolved into a robust communication tool for various teams and projects. It offers text, voice, and video communication across diverse channels, allowing for seamless interaction among team members. Discord's server and channel structure is particularly conducive to managing large teams where members can segment into specific groups according to project needs or departments. This flexibility makes it an excellent option for teams working in remote or hybrid setups, as it supports synchronous and asynchronous communication effectively.

Unity Intercom

Unity Intercom and Unity Cloud are pivotal in enhancing communication for remote productions, providing innovative, accessible, and cost-effective communication solutions on a global scale.

Unity Intercom (local Mac server) offers a robust system for remote communication, supporting up to 128 party line (PL) channels, 64 groups, and 64 external program feed/mix-minus channels, along with person-to-person private communication. It integrates seamlessly with local sound consoles and external communication systems, offering broadcast-quality audio that is essential for effective remote production communication.

Unity Cloud, on the other hand, serves as a simplified, cloud-based alternative to the more feature-rich Unity Intercom system. Ideal for situations where a full-featured, self-hosted system is unnecessary or hosting on a Mac is not feasible, Unity Cloud supports a single group of users sharing six party-line channels. Its setup process is streamlined through an online web portal, making it an accessible option for various remote productions to maintain constant connectivity among team members, regardless of their location.

Unity Intercom is a popular team communications tool for live broadcast.

Together, Unity Intercom and Unity Cloud are reshaping remote production workflows by eliminating geographical barriers and fostering more cohesive and efficient team collaborations.

Zoom

Zoom has become synonymous with remote communication, particularly noted for its video conferencing capabilities. It provides a reliable platform for virtual meetings, webinars, and live chat options. For teams operating in separate locations, Zoom's features like high-quality video, screen sharing, and real-time messaging are indispensable. It ensures that team members remain connected and can collaborate effectively despite geographical distances. Furthermore, Zoom's ability to host large numbers of participants and integrate with multiple calendar systems and workflow tools makes it a preferred choice for corporate and creative environments alike.

Embracing remote production is not merely about adopting new technologies but about rethinking how media is produced and delivered in a digital age. The insights gained from this chapter should serve as a foundation for broadcasters and media professionals to build more resilient, flexible, and creative production capabilities. By doing so, they can not only overcome the logistical and financial challenges associated with traditional production methods but also unlock new opportunities for growth and engagement in an increasingly interconnected world.

KEY TAKEAWAYS FROM THIS CHAPTER:

1. **Customized Workflow Alignment**: In remote production, workflows should align with each team member's skills and tools. When workflows are tailored to specific roles like producers, camera operators, and audio mixers, turnaround times improve, and resources are used more effectively, essential in high-pressure environments.

2. **Role-Specific Requirements**: Each role in a remote production setup has unique requirements. Producers require seamless team coordination, camera operators need integration with remote technologies, color correction specialists need tools for high-fidelity grading, and audio mixers need streamlined audio feed management.

3. **Scalability and Adaptability**: Remote workflows should be scalable to accommodate changing audience sizes and market demands. By remaining adaptable to new technologies and processes, teams can maintain continuous, cost-effective operations in fluctuating circumstances.

4. **Effective Communication Tools**: Collaboration in remote productions relies heavily on tools like Discord, Unity, or Zoom. These facilitate multimedia sharing and real-time feedback, ensuring seamless communication across geographically distributed teams for efficient project execution.

13 REMOTE PRODUCTION SOFTWARE TOOLS

Software tools are the backbone of modern remote production, enabling broadcasters and content creators to execute complex production tasks from afar. These tools offer sophisticated functionalities that traditionally required extensive hardware and physical presence, now streamlined into flexible, scalable, and cost-effective software solutions.

This chapter will review a selection of key software tools used in remote production, divided into six main areas. Each section focuses on different essential tools that enhance remote production capabilities across various broadcasting contexts.

Audio tools such as Cloud MX Audio Mixer, MIXBUS Virtual Broadcast Mixer, and On-Hertz Artisto ensure high-quality sound in remote productions. Cloud MX Audio Mixer stands out for its integration with Waves' renowned eMotion LV1 mix engine, providing pristine audio quality through cloud-based technology, which enhances scalability and reduces operational costs. MIXBUS Virtual Broadcast Mixer caters specifically to live broadcast environments with its user-friendly features that support complex live audio operations. On-Hertz Artisto offers a comprehensive and versatile platform, supporting various broadcasting standards and protocols, ideal for modern broadcasters seeking flexibility and high-quality audio output.

The chapter also discusses advanced contribution tools like Rivet SRT Streaming and VDO.Ninja that address common challenges in remote broadcasting by providing secure, efficient, and user-friendly solutions for live video feeds. Control systems such as Central Control, Bitfocus Companion, and PTZOptics Hive enhance efficiency and manageability in remote production settings, allowing seamless integration and control of production elements.

Furthermore, encoding solutions from Matrox, OBS, and Restream.io are examined for their effectiveness in transforming raw video and audio into formats suitable for streaming and broadcasting. Innovative graphics and visual effects tools like NewBlue Captivate and Singular.Live are also highlighted, illustrating their role in enhancing the visual appeal and interactive capabilities of broadcasts.

Lastly, the chapter looks into switching software and tools such as vMix, CloudMix, Tellyo, Grabyo, and Switcher Studio, which manage multiple video feeds and ensure high-quality production outcomes. This overview not only shows the breadth of technologies available for remote production but also underscores the importance of selecting the right tools to meet specific production needs and enhance broadcasting quality.

7.1 Software Audio Tools

As remote production continues to reshape the landscape of broadcasting, audio tools have evolved to meet the needs of this dynamic sector. Innovations in cloud-based audio mixing and processing technologies have significantly expanded the capabilities available to broadcasters and media networks. This section examines three advanced audio tools that are setting new standards in the industry: Cloud MX Audio Mixer, MIXBUS Virtual Broadcast Mixer (MIXBUS VBM), and On-Hertz Artisto. Each of these tools brings unique features that enhance audio quality, operational flexibility, and scalability, making them pivotal for modern remote productions.

REMOTE PRODUCTION PRO TIP

Cloud MX is a 100% cloud audio mixing tool. Learn more here.

Cloud MX Audio Mixer

The Cloud MX Audio Mixer is a standout for its integration with Waves' renowned eMotion LV1 mix engine, which provides double-precision, 32-bit floating-point audio processing. This capability ensures pristine sound quality that is essential for professional broadcasts. As a completely cloud-based solution, Cloud MX eliminates the need for physical audio equipment, reducing logistical burdens and operational costs. It supports scalability to any production size, seamlessly integrating with major cloud platforms like AWS and Google Cloud Platform, and protocols such as Dante Connect and NDI®, making it versatile for various broadcast environments.

MIXBUS Virtual Broadcast Mixer (MIXBUS VBM)

Harrison's MIXBUS VBM is tailored specifically for live broadcast and corporate communications, offering a broadcast-friendly architecture that includes four dedicated program buses and virtual lobbies for off-air communication among contributors. It also features an automatically generated mix-minus for each contributor, enhancing the clarity and quality of broadcasts. Optimized for NDI and other streaming formats through its flexible plugin architecture, MIXBUS VBM provides robust support for future streaming technologies. Its design prioritizes user interaction, with features like VCA faders for flexible channel grouping and a comprehensive monitoring system, making it an excellent tool for enterprise-scale operations.

MIXBUS is a cloud ready audio mixer from Harrison. Learn more here.

On-Hertz Artisto

On-Hertz Artisto is designed to simplify complex audio production environments. It offers a comprehensive toolbox that breaks away from traditional production limitations, providing a unified platform for all audio needs. Artisto is highly adaptable, supporting a wide array of broadcasting standards and protocols, which allows it to scale seamlessly and maintain audio excellence. Its user-friendly design and comprehensive API ensure easy integration into existing setups, making it ideal for modern broadcasters looking to streamline their operations and enhance production quality.

REMOTE PRODUCTION PRO TIP

On-Hertz Artiso is a cloud-based audio production software. Learn more here.

What about Dante?

If you are working with Dante sources already, the transition to remote production is going to be easier than working with traditional analog systems. Dante Director is a new cloud-based Software as a Service (SaaS) application designed to enhance the management and organization of Dante devices across IP networks. Accessible from any web browser, this application facilitates the proactive monitoring and control of one or more Dante networks.

Dante Director's suite of features includes remote management capabilities that allow users to oversee network operations and monitor device status from any location. This feature is pivotal in maintaining optimal network performance, enabling users to monitor Dante device clocking, connectivity, and latency issues across multiple physical IP networks. The remote control functionality further streamlines operations by permitting the remote launching of Dante Controller to manage, update, and reconfigure Dante device subscriptions. This eliminates the necessity for physical presence, reducing downtime and simplifying configurations.

Dante Director supports remote AV routing. It significantly enhances the efficiency and security of managing audio networks. By providing powerful tools for remote monitoring, control, and organization, along with robust security measures and detailed event logging, Dante Director ensures that audio professionals can maintain high standards of audio quality and network reliability from anywhere in the world. This makes Dante Director an indispensable tool for modern audio professionals looking to optimize their network operations.

REMOTE PRODUCTION
PRO TIP

Dante is an IP based audio system from Audinate. Learn more here.

IP based audio has come a long way over the years. In the next chapter, we will also cover remote production for hardware based audio mixers as well. While audio mixing has never been the easiest part of an overall video production it is usually the most important part. Carefully consider your audio workflow to make sure it can support your remote production needs.

7.2 Video Contribution Tools

In the realm of remote production, contribution tools are essential for capturing and transmitting high-quality video and audio feeds from various locations back to the production studio or directly to audiences.

Remote Production

This section explores a range of innovative contribution tools that address common challenges in remote broadcasting by providing secure, efficient, and user-friendly solutions. These tools include Epiphan Pearl (covered in the hardware chapter), Rivet SRT Streaming, VDO.Ninja, LiveU backpack-based encoders, Zoom Video Meetings, and Larix Broadcaster, each offering unique capabilities to enhance live production workflows.

Rivet SRT Streaming

Rivet SRT Streaming leverages Secure Reliable Transport (SRT), a cutting-edge streaming protocol designed to overcome the challenges of low-latency and high-quality video over unpredictable networks. SRT is crucial for remote production as it optimizes streaming performance across congested networks by adapting to varying bandwidth availability and minimizing potential disruptions caused by network congestion. This technology ensures that broadcasters can deliver uninterrupted, broadcast-grade quality video, even under adverse conditions. Rivet SRT Streaming, therefore, becomes an indispensable tool for professionals needing reliable and secure video streaming solutions that maintain integrity and quality regardless of the transmission environment.

Rivet is a remote streaming tool designed for SRT. Learn more here.

VDO.Ninja

VDO.Ninja dramatically simplifies the process of bringing remote video feeds into production workflows by utilizing browser-based technology. This tool allows contributors to send live video feeds directly from their web browsers without the need for any additional software installation. The ease of use and accessibility of VDO.Ninja make it an excellent choice for productions where time and ease of setup are critical. It is particularly useful in scenarios such as quickly organized live events, remote interviews, and multi-location broadcasts, offering production teams the flexibility to include a variety of video sources seamlessly into their projects.

REMOTE PRODUCTION PRO TIP

VDO.ninja is free tool for adding remote guests to your production. Learn more here.

The capabilities and applications of these tools demonstrate their importance in modern broadcasting environments, where the demand for high-quality, reliable, and accessible video contribution solutions is continuously growing. By enabling secure, efficient, and scalable video streaming and contributions, Rivet SRT Streaming and VDO.Ninja help broadcasters meet these demands, ensuring that production quality is maintained irrespective of the logistical and technical challenges posed by remote setups.

Hive-Linked Cameras

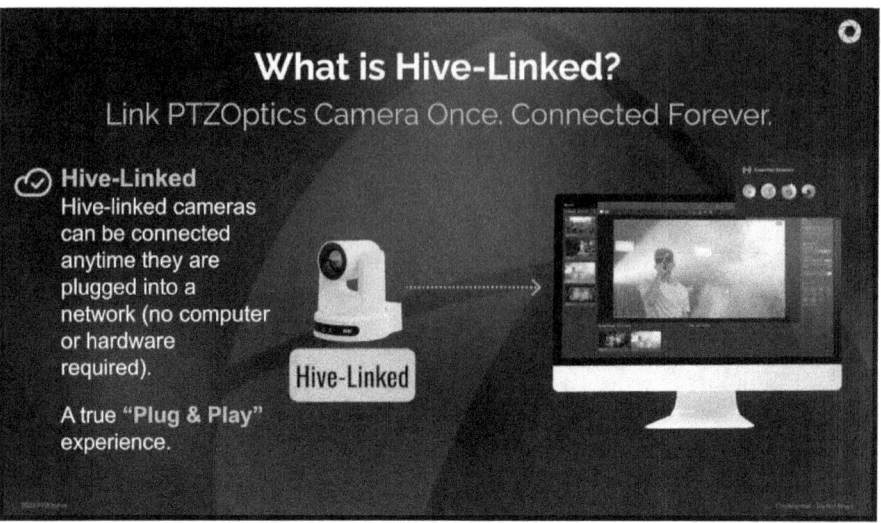

Hive-Linked cameras are able to be connected directly to a Hive studio one time and forever become an edge device for connection back to that Hive Studio. A Hive Studio is a cloud-based video production solution designed for cinematic PTZ camera controls, video switching, recording and streaming. To set up a Hive-Linked camera you will need to login to the camera's web-interface and connect the camera to your Hive Studio. You can do this by logging into your Hive account and selecting the Studio you would like the camera to be connected to. Once connected, the camera will always connect to this studio when it boots up and is connected to the internet. In this way, Hive-Linked cameras are ideal for remote productions, where equipment is either pre-installed or shipped directly to the remote site.

Hive also supports over 400 PTZ cameras that are not "Hive-Linked." The difference is that standard IP-connected PTZ cameras will require the Hive software running on a computer on the LAN. The Hive software is able to act as the bridge between the LAN and the cloud allowing for low-latency remote production with a wide range of PTZ cameras.

Larix Broadcaster

Larix Broadcaster is a smartphone app designed for remote production, especially useful in journalism and sports broadcasting where high-quality, real-time streaming is crucial. This free-to-use mobile application by Softvelum is available for both Android and iOS platforms and offers a straightforward, reliable solution for live streaming directly from mobile devices. It supports multiple streaming protocols such as RTMP, RTMPS, SRT, RIST, and Icecast, facilitating broadcasts to nearly any platform or server.

With its ability to stream in high-definition, Larix Broadcaster ensures that audiences receive the best possible viewing experience, even when broadcasters are operating from remote or dynamic environments like sports fields or breaking news locations. The app's user-friendly interface allows even novice users to start streaming quickly and effortlessly with just a few taps.

For sports journalists and remote reporters, Larix Broadcaster proves particularly beneficial. It enables live interviews with athletes or coaches from virtually anywhere, be it inside dressing rooms or on the pitch. Reporters covering various events, from press conferences to natural disasters, can also leverage this tool to provide instant live coverage to their audience. The versatility and protocol support of Larix Broadcaster mean content can be shared across multiple platforms simultaneously, making it an essential, cost-effective tool for delivering engaging, live content in the digital age of journalism and sports broadcasting.

REMOTE PRODUCTION PRO TIP

Larix Broadcaster is a smartphone app for broadcasting video. Learn more here.

LiveU Backpacks

LiveU battery powered cellular-bonding encoder backpacks represent a robust solution for live video transmission. This advanced technology combines multiple cellular connections into a single robust connection, ensuring reliable and high-quality video streams even from remote or challenging locations. LiveU backpacks are designed to be lightweight and portable, making them ideal for on-the-go broadcasting scenarios such as breaking news, outdoor events, and sports broadcasting. Their resilience and ability to deliver stable live HD feeds under variable network conditions make them a staple in modern field reporting and live broadcasting, where mobility and reliability are paramount.

LiveU has realized the importance of cloud-based production in their customer workflows, and launched LiveU Studio shortly after acquiring EasyLive. LiveU Studio is a complete cloud-based video switching and streaming service that is designed to work seamlessly with their backpacks.

REMOTE PRODUCTION
PRO TIP

LiveU is a cellular bonding technology provider. Learn more here.

Together, LiveU backpacks, Zoom, and Larix Broadcaster exemplify the versatility and adaptability of modern contribution tools in remote production environments. Each tool provides unique solutions that address specific needs within the broadcasting process, from mobile, high-quality field transmissions to integrating remote interviews and guest appearances into live broadcasts. These tools not only enhance the operational flexibility of remote productions but also ensure that high production values are maintained, regardless of the logistical challenges. As remote production continues to evolve, the role of these innovative contribution tools will be crucial in shaping the future of broadcasting, enabling producers to deliver engaging, high-quality content to audiences worldwide.

7.3 Control Systems

In the dynamic realm of remote production, control systems play a crucial role in streamlining operations and integrating various production elements seamlessly. This section focuses on three advanced control systems: Central Control, Bitfocus Companion, and PTZOptics Hive, each offering unique functionalities to enhance the efficiency and capabilities of remote production environments.

Once the foundational elements are established, the next step involves streamlining the workflow for operators, which often includes the integration of a control surface. While large-scale setups like Viz Vectar come equipped with extensive control surfaces designed for specific inputs and workflows, there are more adaptable options available that can effectively turn a laptop into a professional remote production hub.

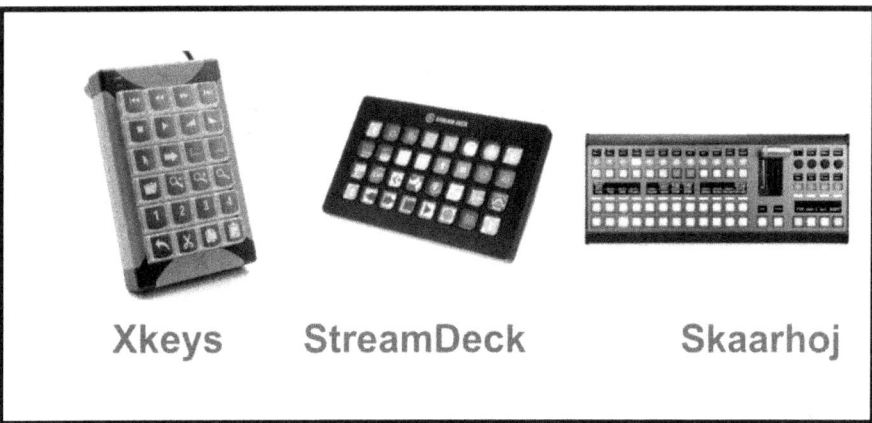

Various programmable control surfaces for production operations.

Among various control surfaces, options like P.I. Engineering's X-keys, Skaarhoj's advanced control devices, Elgato's StreamDeck and MIDI controllers are available. Each offers customizable functionality, allowing users to define what each button does and adjust settings between shows. Notably, Elgato's Stream Deck stands out for its simplicity and elegance, providing a versatile and easy-to-use interface ideal for remote production environments. The Stream Deck, along with its mobile version, enables producers to use additional programmable buttons from an old phone, enhancing accessibility and convenience.

These tools often come with proprietary software, but there are also third-party solutions mentioned earlier in this book such as Central Control and Bitfocus Companion that act as the "middleware", integrating various controllers with desired software and hardware.

Central Control

Central Control offers a comprehensive solution for managing a wide array of devices and software used in production, from video mixers and graphics systems to lighting consoles and PTZ cameras. It supports over 50+ different controllers, including MIDI, X-keys, and Stream Deck, making it a versatile choice for complex production setups. Key features include a timeline-based macro editor for automating complex sequences, an innovative show rundown system that caters to both volunteers and TV professionals, and a teleprompter with NDI output. Central Control also facilitates quick mapping of practically any MIDI controller to live production devices, simplifying the process of integrating new hardware into existing workflows.

REMOTE PRODUCTION PRO TIP

Central Control is a video production control software company. Learn more here.

Central Control used with a virtual vMix instance

Central Control allows for remote operation of applications like vMix running in the cloud by simply inputting the IP address of the vMix instance. This flexibility extends to managing multiple controllers, enabling different operators to handle various aspects of the production, such as switching inputs or controlling overlays and streams using devices like the Akai APC Mini and Stream Deck.

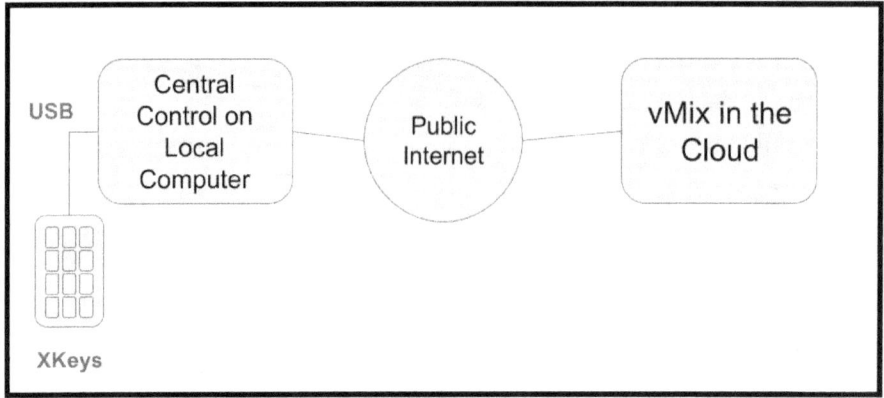

Simple workflow showing Central Control used to control a vMix server running in the cloud.

Central Control is especially beneficial in setups involving cloud instances, where traditionally connecting USB devices is unavailable. Setup involves downloading Central Control, connecting devices via USB or a network, and then adding these devices within the software. Users can then customize button feedback and assign specific commands to different keys, simplifying the control process.

Central Control's ability to integrate with multiple IP networks simultaneously enhances its utility. For instance, managing multiple vMix instances and local switchers from a single controller like the Stream Deck XL demonstrates its capacity to centralize control, making management of complex setups straightforward. Moreover, it supports protocol conversion, allowing diverse control devices to interact seamlessly across different communication standards.

At $50 USD, Central Control offers a cost-effective solution that significantly enhances the flexibility and efficiency of remote production workflows, making it an invaluable tool for those looking to streamline their production processes.

Bitfocus Companion

Bitfocus Companion transforms the affordable Elgato Stream Deck into a professional control surface suitable for managing a wide range of presentation switchers, video playback software and broadcast equipment. Companion doesn't require physical Stream Deck hardware to operate; it includes a built-in emulator, a web interface for touch screens (including tablets and phones), and the capability to trigger functions via OSC, TCP, UDP, HTTP (includingAPIs), WebSocket and ArtNet. Its features include a button designer for personalized control layouts, feedback from devices to display button states, stacked actions, delayed actions, and the ability to manage multiple Stream Decks simultaneously (even from other Stream Decks). This flexibility makes it an ideal tool for simplifying complex processes within remote production environments.

REMOTE PRODUCTION
PRO TIP

Bitfocus Companion is an open-source control project. Learn more here.

White Label Webcasting uses Companion with 4 Stream Decks (controlled by a 5th) to operate Vmix, 5 PTZOptics cameras, 2 MultiViews, an 80x80 routing switcher, 8 Hyperdecks and Unity Intercom.

PTZOptics Hive

PTZOptics Hive focuses on enhancing the control of PTZ cameras, crucial for remote productions that utilize robotic cameras. Hive allows real-time collaboration and streamlined workflows, enabling users to manage camera settings from anywhere in the world with sub-300 ms latency. Its features include advanced framing and color correction tools, auto-tracking capabilities that work with any brand of PTZ camera, and unlimited custom presets for organizing camera shots. Hive is embedded in PTZOptics cameras, facilitating instant cloud control without the need for additional hardware. This integration makes it an invaluable tool for achieving cinematic control and managing multi-studio setups remotely.

REMOTE PRODUCTION
PRO TIP

PTZOptics Hive is free to use with one camera. You can learn more about this remote production software here.

Central Control, Bitfocus Companion, and PTZOptics Hive each provide unique solutions to the challenges of remote production, offering tools that enhance control, simplify operations, and ensure high-quality outputs. Whether through advanced automation capabilities, customizable control interfaces, or specialized camera management features, these systems are pivotal in transforming remote production workflows, making them more efficient and adaptable to various production demands. These control systems not only streamline the technical aspects of production but also empower creative teams to execute their visions effectively, regardless of geographical constraints.

7.4 Software Encoders

Encoding solutions are essential in remote production for converting raw video and audio inputs into digital formats suitable for streaming or broadcasting over the Internet. This section discusses three powerful tools: OBS, Restream.io, and vMix, each providing unique capabilities to enhance the streaming and broadcasting workflows. In the next chapter, we will review hardware-based encoders for remote production.

OBS (Open Broadcaster Software)

OBS is a versatile, open-source software widely used for video recording and live streaming. It is favored for its high flexibility and extensive feature set, which includes support for multiple sources, scenes, and transitions, as well as robust settings for audio mixing and video encoding. OBS allows users to create professional quality broadcasts by combining various media sources and applying real-time audio and video effects. Its open-source nature not only makes it free to use but also continuously evolving thanks to contributions from a global developer community.

Several new services are available to help users deploy OBS instances in the cloud including v2Cloud and StreamingServer.io . To host OBS Studio on a cloud server effectively, you'll need a server with robust processing capabilities. Video encoding demands significant CPU power, and the specific requirements will depend on your target resolution, frame rate, and bitrate. Additionally, if you're incorporating live feeds into your OBS instance—common in IRL streaming—sufficient GPU power is essential to decode incoming streams smoothly. For optimal performance in both encoding and decoding, a server equipped with a dedicated GPU is recommended. Installing OBS Studio on a cloud server involves similar steps to a local setup, though specifics can vary based on the server's operating system (Windows or Linux) and the hardware configuration. It's crucial to ensure that all drivers, especially those needed for hardware acceleration, are correctly installed before starting OBS.

REMOTE PRODUCTION PRO TIP

OBS is a live streaming and video production software. Learn more here.

REMOTE PRODUCTION PRO TIP

Restream.io is a cloud-based restreaming service. Learn more here.

Restream.io

Restream.io is a powerful multi-streaming service that enables users to broadcast live content to over 30 streaming platforms simultaneously, including YouTube, Twitch, Facebook, and LinkedIn. This service is particularly useful for content creators and marketers looking to maximize their audience reach across different platforms without the need for multiple streaming setups. Restream.io also offers chat aggregation, analytics, and scheduling features, making it a comprehensive tool for managing and optimizing live streaming efforts.

vMix

vMix is a popular live streaming software solution that can now be deployed in cloud environments, such as Amazon EC2, for enhanced scalability and accessibility.

vMix has been one of the most reliable and popular live streaming software solutions for years, and was originally designed for in-studio production. Over the years, vMix has grown its feature set and pioneered integrations with NDI for IP based video production and Zoom. When it comes to remote production, vMix can be used on-premise or in the cloud as a solution to receive and mix remote video feeds.

REMOTE PRODUCTION
PRO TIP

vMix is a live streaming software. Learn more here.

You can learn more about Vmix in the Cloud in Chapter 10, Advanced Topics in Remote Production.

Viz Vectar Plus

Viz Vectar Plus is an innovative, cloud-based production switcher that stands out in the field. Designed to be intuitive and flexible, Viz Vectar Plus offers a user-friendly interface that caters to professionals looking to streamline their broadcasting workflows. Unlike traditional hardware-dependent setups, its cloud-based nature allows for operation without the need for specific hardware, giving users the freedom to manage and execute productions from virtually any location.

REMOTE PRODUCTION PRO TIP

Viz Vectar Plus is a software driven live streaming solution. Learn more here.

This flexibility makes Viz Vectar Plus especially suitable for productions that require rapid deployment or operate across multiple locations. Additionally, the platform supports a variety of input sources and integrates seamlessly with other media systems, making it a versatile choice for live broadcasts, whether for news, sports, or entertainment events. As broadcasting continues to evolve with technological advancements, Viz Vectar Plus represents a forward-thinking solution that adapts to the dynamic needs of modern producers and broadcasters.

The shift towards software-based vision mixers, featuring tools like OBS, vMix, Wirecast, and Viz Vectar Plus, has revolutionized video production and broadcasting by enhancing flexibility, cost-effectiveness, and accessibility.

The real game changer in professional broadcasting is the implementation of High Availability (HA) configurations. HA setups ensure reliability by using redundant systems, allowing for immediate takeover if one system fails, thus maintaining uninterrupted service.

This is crucial for maintaining professional broadcast quality and reliability across any of the mentioned software tools.

As we look to the future, the role of software-based vision mixers is set to grow even more prominent. With the increasing trend towards remote work and digital collaboration, these tools' capability to be deployed and accessed from anywhere further positions them as essential assets in the evolving broadcasting landscape.

The industry's pivot to software-based vision mixers like OBS, vMix, Wirecast, and Viz Vectar Plus, especially when combined with high availability configurations, marks a new era in broadcasting. This shift not only democratizes production, making it accessible to more creators, but also ensures that broadcasts can be delivered with high reliability and quality. As a proponent and user of vMix, I can affirm its significant, transformative impact on broadcasting, empowering both seasoned professionals and newcomers to step confidently into the future of media production.

7.5 Live Graphics, Captioning and Translation

In remote production, graphics and visual effects play an important role in enhancing the viewer experience and delivering professionally polished broadcasts. This section discusses two advanced tools, NewBlue Captivate and Singular.Live, which provide dynamic and innovative solutions for creating and managing graphics in live production environments. Many of the all-in-one cloud production solutions from Ross, Chyron and Vizrt have production graphics built into their overall solution. NewBlue and Singluar.Live are software solutions you can use to bolt-on to your existing production system.

NewBlue Captivate

NewBlue Captivate is a comprehensive tool designed for creating dynamic on-screen graphics that capture the audience's attention. It offers a wide range of features that enable broadcasters to design and implement graphics that are not only visually appealing but also contextually relevant to the content being presented. Whether for news tickers, lower-thirds, or full-screen graphics, NewBlue Captivate provides an array of customizable templates and real-time animation capabilities that enhance any broadcast.

The strength of NewBlue Captivate lies in its ability to integrate seamlessly with existing production workflows, allowing for quick changes and updates to graphics on the fly. This flexibility is crucial during live events where information can change rapidly, and broadcasts need to remain accurate and current. The software supports a variety of input options and can synchronize with databases or RSS feeds to automatically update content, ensuring that viewers receive the most up-to-date information.

REMOTE PRODUCTION PRO TIP

NewBlueFX is a live streaming and graphics

REMOTE PRODUCTION PRO TIP

Singular.Live is a cloud-based graphics solution. Learn more here.

Singular.Live

Singular.Live offers a cloud-based graphics platform specifically tailored for live productions. It allows users to create and control broadcast-quality graphics directly from a web browser, eliminating the need for specialized hardware. This platform is particularly well-suited for productions that require a high degree of scalability and flexibility, as it can be accessed from anywhere in the world, making it ideal for remote and distributed teams.

One of the key features of Singular.Live is its ability to adapt graphics in real-time based on incoming data and viewer interactions. This responsiveness makes it an excellent choice for sports broadcasts, election coverage, and any other live event where data changes moment-to-moment. Additionally, Singular.Live supports collaborative workflows, enabling multiple users to work on the same project simultaneously, which enhances productivity and streamlines the graphics creation process.

Live Captioning with CloudFlowHub by Cinedeck

CloudFlow Hub, developed by Cinedeck, represents a significant advancement in cloud-based video production and distribution. Integrating functionalities from their established products—CD2, cineXtools, and Connex—CloudFlow Hub offers a unified platform that enhances media production workflows. It is particularly noted for its AI-enhanced live captioning capabilities, making it an all-in-one solution for media producers. This allows you to ingest SRT video feeds and "Rewrap" the video with AI transcriptions and translation. This is ideal for live playout in television and broadcast who cater to multiple languages.

Both NewBlue Captivate and Singular.Live provide powerful, flexible solutions for incorporating graphics and visual effects into live broadcasts. NewBlue Captivate excels in offering broadcasters a robust set of tools for creating customizable, animated graphics that enhance storytelling and viewer engagement. On the other hand, Singular.Live brings both an easy, customizable template-based interface as well as it's more complex, fully capable After Effects like "Composer" interface Together, these tools address the diverse needs of today's broadcasters, ensuring that they can deliver visually compelling and informative content to their audiences.

7.6 Video Switching

In the realm of remote production, switching software and tools are fundamental to managing multiple video feeds, ensuring seamless transitions between scenes, and enhancing overall production quality. This section explores a range of cutting-edge solutions that cater to different aspects of live production and streaming, including vMix, CloudMix, Tellyo, Grabyo, Switcher Studio, and Hive.

vMix

As mentioned earlier, vMix is a truly comprehensive software solution designed for live production and streaming. It offers a rich set of features including live mixing, switching, recording, and live streaming of SD, full HD, and 4K video sources. vMix is known for its high-performance live production capabilities, providing users with the tools to produce professional-quality broadcasts on a relatively modest budget. vMix starts at just $60 for the Basic HD version. You can get a free 60 day trial to test its capabilities with your workflow.

CloudMix

CloudMix is a cloud-native solution that enables producers to mix live feeds and add graphics from anywhere in the world. This platform leverages cloud technology to provide scalability and accessibility, allowing users to manage live productions without the need for heavy hardware investments. CloudMix is ideal for distributed teams and events that require coordination across multiple locations, offering a

REMOTE PRODUCTION PRO TIP

CloudMix is a live streaming software. Learn more here.

flexible and efficient production environment. CloudMix has a specific focus on musicians and provides solutions for making money with fan/creator connections.

Tellyo

Tellyo is a streaming solution that has developed to also include post-production tools for video editing. Its platform supports real-time video editing, clipping, and distribution, making it an excellent tool for sports events, news, and other live scenarios where speed and responsiveness are critical. Tellyo enhances the capabilities of production teams to capture, edit, and share video content across various platforms instantaneously.

Grabyo

Grabyo is another cloud native video production tool with integrated video editing. It provides tools for live production, video editing, and social media distribution, all from within a cloud-based interface that can be accessed globally. Grabyo's strength lies in its ability to quickly adapt to the fast-paced nature of live broadcasting and digital content strategies, making it a valuable tool for media companies looking to streamline their workflows and enhance audience engagement.

Grabyo is a cloud-based video production software. Learn more here.

PTZOptics Hive

Hive is not only about PTZ camera control but will soon (as of this writing) offer robust live switching capabilities. Hive integrates seamlessly with over 400 PTZ cameras to provide a unified platform for controlling camera movements and switching between feeds, enhancing live production with its real-time collaboration features. Its cloud-based infrastructure enables producers to manage productions remotely with precision and ease, making it suitable for a wide range of broadcast scenarios. Hive stands out with its role-based studio sharing capabilities allowing teams to span the globe with specific access to the video production tools necessary for each team member.

PTZOptics Hive is free to use with one camera. You can learn more about this remote production software here.

Conclusion

The range of switching software and tools like vMix, CloudMix, Tellyo, Grabyo, and PTZOptics Hive provides comprehensive solutions that meet the diverse needs of today's live production environments. From traditional software-based mixers to innovative cloud-native platforms and mobile solutions, these tools ensure that producers can create dynamic, engaging, and professional broadcasts regardless of their location or the complexity of their production needs.

KEY TAKEAWAYS FROM THIS CHAPTER:

1. **Software Tools Enable Remote Production**: Software solutions are essential in modern remote production, replacing traditional hardware to provide broadcasters and content creators with scalable,

flexible, and cost-effective tools.

2. **Key Audio and Contribution Tools**: Audio tools like Cloud MX Audio Mixer, MIXBUS Virtual Broadcast Mixer, and On-Hertz Artisto ensure high-quality sound. Contribution tools, including Rivet SRT Streaming and VDO.Ninja, offer secure and efficient solutions for live video feeds.

3. **Control and Encoding Systems**: Control systems like Central Control and Bitfocus Companion streamline device management, while encoding solutions like Matrox, OBS, and Restream.io transform raw media into broadcast-ready formats.

4. **Graphics and Vision Mixers**: Innovative graphics tools, like NewBlue Captivate and Singular.Live, enhance broadcast visuals. Software-based vision mixers (OBS, vMix) democratize broadcasting, offering reliability and quality to all creators.

14 REMOTE PRODUCTION HARDWARE TOOLS

This chapter will delve into the essential hardware components necessary for remote production, providing a comprehensive guide to the technology that powers professional broadcasts from various locations. We will explore each category of hardware—PTZ cameras, encoders, decoders, controllers, networking equipment, and audio mixers—highlighting their functionalities, advantages, and how they integrate into broader production workflows.

The Role of Hardware in Remote Production

Remote production hardware encompasses a wide range of equipment, from cameras and audio mixers to encoders, decoders, and networking devices. Each piece of hardware plays a pivotal role in capturing, processing, and transmitting audio-visual content, ensuring that it can be broadcasted seamlessly to audiences regardless of geographic boundaries. As the demand for live and on-demand content increases, the reliance on sophisticated remote production hardware becomes more pronounced, driving innovations that cater to the needs of modern broadcasters.

Enhancing Capabilities and Flexibility

Advances in hardware technology have significantly expanded the capabilities and flexibility of remote productions. Modern PTZ cameras, for example, offer remote controllability and high-quality video output, making them ideal for dynamic shooting environments where quick adjustments are necessary. Similarly, contemporary encoders and decoders provide efficient video compression and decompression, ensuring that high-definition streams can be delivered even over limited bandwidth

Moreover, the integration of cloud technologies with traditional hardware setups has opened new avenues for remote control and management of production equipment, allowing crews to operate equipment from distant locations via the internet. This level of flexibility is crucial for productions that require rapid deployment and scalability, such as news broadcasting and live sports events.

8.1 PTZ Cameras for Remote Production

Pan-Tilt-Zoom (PTZ) cameras are essential tools in the arsenal of modern remote production, offering a combination of high-quality video output and versatile remote controllability. Their integration into production setups significantly enhances the flexibility and efficiency of broadcasting, particularly in dynamic environments where quick adjustments are crucial.

Networking and Configuration

PTZ cameras are typically connected to a network, which allows for remote operation and management. To ensure reliable and consistent connectivity, it is ideal to assign a static IP address to each camera. This setup prevents IP conflicts and ensures that the cameras are easily accessible over the network at all times, regardless of network changes or restarts.

Power and Control

One of the significant advantages of modern PTZ cameras is their ability to be powered over Ethernet (PoE). This capability simplifies installation and reduces cable clutter by allowing both power and data connections to be handled by a single Ethernet cable. Moreover, PoE enables cameras to be installed in locations where traditional power outlets are unavailable or hard to reach.

Enhanced Features with NDI

Network Device Interface (NDI) significantly expands the capabilities of PTZ cameras beyond mere video output. NDI allows PTZ cameras to transmit high-quality video over a network with low latency, making it ideal for live productions. Additionally, NDI supports the integration of tally lights, providing visual cues to talent about which camera is live, and includes audio transmission capabilities, thereby simplifying the audio setup in multi-camera environments.

Remote Control Options

Remote control of PTZ cameras is facilitated through various devices, including dedicated joystick controllers like the PTZOptics SuperJoy. These controllers are often integrated with NDI, allowing for seamless control of camera movements, zoom, and focus, enhancing the operator's ability to make adjustments on the fly during live broadcasts. The SuperJoy controller, for example, offers a user-friendly interface and extensive functionality, making it an excellent choice for productions that require precise camera control.

Cloud-Ready Solutions with Hive-Linked Cameras

PTZOptics has pioneered cloud-ready solutions with its Hive-Linked cameras, such as the PTZOptics Move SE, Move 4K and Link 4K models. These cameras are designed to be directly connected to the cloud, enabling remote deployment and control. This feature is particularly valuable in scenarios where cameras need to be shipped to remote locations and set up for immediate use without complicated configuration. Once connected to the cloud system, these cameras can be managed and controlled from anywhere, providing tremendous flexibility and scalability for remote productions.

PTZ cameras are transforming remote production by combining high-quality video output with advanced networking and control features. The use of static IP addresses and PoE simplifies their installation and integration into existing networks. NDI technology enhances their functionality by supporting video, audio, and tally light integration over a network. Additionally, innovations like NDI-integrated controllers and cloud-ready PTZ cameras offer unprecedented control and flexibility, allowing production teams to manage remote events effectively. These capabilities make PTZ cameras an indispensable part of modern broadcasting, catering to the needs of a dynamic and evolving media landscape.

8.2 Hardware for Encoding and Decoding

In the realm of remote production, encoders play a critical role in ensuring that video and audio content is suitably formatted for transmission over the internet. To understand their importance, it's helpful to distinguish between encoders and their counterparts, decoders.

Understanding Encoders and Decoders

Encoders are devices or software that convert video and audio content from raw formats into digital formats that are easier to transmit over networks and the internet. This process includes compressing the content and encoding it into a streamable format, such as H.264 or H.265 (aka HEVC), which are commonly used for efficient video compression.

Decoders, on the other hand, perform the reverse operation. They take the encoded data received over the network and convert it back into a format that can be displayed on screens or played through speakers. This process is essential for the audience on the receiving end to view or listen to the content as intended.

Epiphan Pearl Encoders

The Epiphan Pearl family of encoders stands out as a powerful all-in-one solution for live video production, providing centralized remote management and control for seamless integration into any production environment. With its robust features such as automated streaming and recording scheduling, real-time device monitoring, and cloud collaboration, Pearl simplifies complex production tasks and ensures high-quality output. The platform supports the SRT protocol for low-latency streaming, making it ideal for hybrid and virtual events. Additionally, Epiphan Edge enhances Pearl systems by offering centralized fleet management and ultra efficient batch actions, reducing the legwork in managing multiple devices. Whether used for corporate events, live performances, or educational sessions, Epiphan Pearl delivers a comprehensive and scalable solution for modern remote production needs.

Epiphan Pearl's are remotely manageable production systems.

Magewell Cloud - Centralized Management Software

One of the notable advancements in encoding technology is the development of centralized management software for encoders and other related devices. An excellent example is Magewell's Control Hub software, which supports a range of hardware products including the Ultra Stream and Ultra Encode live media encoders, Pro Convert NDI® encoders and decoders, and more. This software allows users to configure device parameters remotely, trigger operational functions, and upgrade firmware across multiple devices simultaneously. The intuitive dashboard of the Control Hub makes it straightforward for users to monitor the status of their devices and manage deployments efficiently.

Stream Conversion Capabilities

The Magewell Control Hub excels in its ability to convert between multiple streaming protocols. With a flexible stream routing architecture, users can define 'channels' that map an input to one or more output protocols and destinations. This capability enables the conversion of streams between RTMP, SRT, RTSP, and transport streams delivered over UDP or RTP, enhancing the versatility of broadcast workflows.

Kiloview Centralized Management

Similarly, Kiloview offers the KiloLink Server Free, a centralized management platform that leverages KiloLink technology to optimize IP-based video transmission. This platform provides tools for remotely managing KILOVIEW products, allowing users to upgrade, restore, reset, or restart devices with just a few clicks. Additionally, the KILOVIEW Intercom Server (KIS) facilitates multi-channel communication across KILOVIEW products and browsers, supporting up to 32 terminals with nearly zero latency. This system is highly adaptable to various IP-based video transmission workflows, making it a valuable tool for managing communications in on-site or hybrid production environments.

Matrox ORIGIN

Matrox encoders, particularly through the Matrox ORIGIN asynchronous media framework, represent a significant advancement in cloud-based media production. Built on a cloud-native architecture, Matrox ORIGIN specifically addresses the unique challenges of Tier 1 live production environments which demand frame-accurate, deterministic, low latency, redundant, and responsive interconnected systems at scale.

The transition to cloud technologies has been transformative across various sectors of the media industry, enhancing workflows in areas like Media Asset Management (MAM), playout, distribution, archiving, and more. Matrox ORIGIN extends these benefits to live production, a domain where the cloud's impact has been constrained by specific technical demands. By reconciling live production requirements with cloud capabilities, ORIGIN transforms potential technical hurdles into substantial technical and business advantages for developers and broadcasters alike.

Matrox offers hardware encoders for remote production. Learn more here.

Encoders and centralized management platforms like Magewell's Control Hub, Kiloview's KiloLink and Matrox ORIGIN are indispensable in modern remote production setups. They not only streamline the encoding and management processes but also enhance the flexibility and efficiency of broadcasting operations. By providing powerful tools for managing and converting streams, these technologies ensure that producers can maintain high-quality broadcasts and adapt quickly to the dynamic demands of remote production.

8.3 Controllers

xKeys and StreamDeck controllers are invaluable tools for remote production, enhancing efficiency, control, and user experience. These devices offer customizable buttons and keys, allowing producers to create tailored workflows that simplify complex tasks.

xKeys Controllers: Known for their robust build and versatility, xKeys controllers can be programmed to handle various functions such as switching camera angles, adjusting audio levels, and controlling PTZ cameras. Their tactile feedback and reliability make them a favorite for live production environments, where precision and speed are crucial.

StreamDeck Controllers: StreamDecks offer a highly intuitive interface with LCD keys that can display custom icons and information. This visual feedback helps operators quickly identify and execute commands, making it easier to manage multiple aspects of a production. The StreamDeck's integration with various software and platforms further enhances its utility, allowing seamless control over streaming software, video switching, and more.

Both xKeys and StreamDeck controllers significantly streamline remote production workflows, enabling producers to maintain high production quality while managing complex setups remotely. Their user-friendly designs and adaptability to different production needs make them essential tools in modern remote production environments.

8.4 Networking Equipment

Networking Equipment in Remote Production

Networking equipment is fundamental to the success of remote production, serving as the backbone for connecting and transmitting data across multiple production locations. This section explores the critical role of such hardware, focusing on essential components like routers, switches, and modems, and providing configuration tips to ensure a robust network setup. Special attention is given to Netgear Pro AV switches, particularly the M4250 series, which are designed to facilitate advanced AV over IP workflows.

Importance of Networking Hardware

In remote production, networking hardware ensures that audio and video data are efficiently transmitted between various devices and locations without loss or significant delay. The quality of the network setup directly impacts the reliability and quality of the live production, making robust networking equipment essential for maintaining high standards of broadcast integrity and continuity.

Key Components of Networking in Remote Production

Routers, switches, and modems play essential roles in the management and direction of data across networks. Routers are crucial for directing traffic between different networks; they manage the flow of data between the internet and local networks, ensuring that information is efficiently routed to its intended destination. Switches, particularly vital in AV over IP setups, handle data within a local network. They receive, process, and forward data to the appropriate device. For example, switches like the Netgear Pro AV M4250 are specifically optimized for handling high-bandwidth video and audio data, supporting the demands of complex live production environments. Modems serve as the bridge that connects networks to the internet, converting data from the digital formats used by computers to the analog signals utilized over telephone lines or cable systems, facilitating online communication and data transfer.

Netgear Pro AV Switches and NDI Integration

Netgear's commitment to the Pro AV industry is exemplified by their M4250 series switches, which are specifically engineered to support AV over IP applications, including the increasingly popular NDI (Network

Device Interface) protocol. NDI allows for high-quality, low-latency video and audio to be shared across an IP network, which is critical for live production workflows.

The Netgear M4250 switches come with a unique configuration profile for NDI, facilitating instant setup and integration with NDI-compatible devices. This integration is crucial for environments like broadcast studios, houses of worship, and corporate AV setups, where seamless AV over IP workflows are necessary. These switches support the latest NDI 5 codec, enhancing compatibility with a broad range of devices and reducing the complexity traditionally associated with IP-based workflows.

Configuration Tips for Robust Network Setup

Setting up a robust network for remote production requires adherence to several best practices to ensure efficiency and security. Firstly, utilizing profile-based configuration can greatly simplify the network setup. For instance, using switches like the Netgear M4250 enables easy configuration through pre-set profiles that are tailored for specific codecs and applications, ensuring that all necessary settings are correctly applied for optimal performance. Secondly, it is crucial to prioritize network security and stability. This involves implementing strong security protocols and designing your network infrastructure to handle high data loads, which is particularly important for live video and audio transmission. Lastly, maintaining the health and security of your network requires regular firmware updates and monitoring. Keeping all networking equipment updated with the latest firmware helps protect against vulnerabilities, and regularly monitoring network performance allows you to preempt issues before they can impact production.

Networking equipment plays a pivotal role in remote production by ensuring seamless connectivity and data transmission across multiple locations. With advanced solutions like the Netgear Pro AV switches and the integration of protocols such as NDI, production teams can achieve professional-grade AV over IP workflows that are both scalable and efficient. The right setup not only supports the technical demands of remote production but also enhances the overall production quality, making it essential for broadcasters to invest in and maintain robust networking solutions.

8.4 Audio Mixers for Remote Production

Audio Mixers in Remote Production

Audio mixers are a cornerstone of broadcast production, playing a crucial role in ensuring that audio signals are expertly managed and integrated into a seamless output for viewers and listeners. This section explores the functionality of audio mixers in broadcast environments, delves into their advanced features, and provides guidance on selecting the right mixer for various production needs.

Functionality in Broadcast

In the context of remote production, an audio mixer's primary function is to consolidate multiple audio signals from various sources—microphones, soundtracks, instruments, and other inputs—into a single coherent output. This process involves not only combining these inputs but also adjusting levels, tonal qualities, and dynamics to ensure a balanced mix that complements the visual elements of the broadcast. Effective use of an audio mixer is vital in live broadcasts and recorded productions alike, as it affects the clarity and impact of the program's audio content.

Advanced Features of Audio Mixers

Modern audio mixers come equipped with a host of sophisticated features that enhance their functionality and adaptability in complex production scenarios:

- **Multi-Bus Mixing**: This feature allows audio engineers to route audio signals to multiple outputs, or "buses," each with independent controls. This is particularly useful in scenarios where different mixes are required simultaneously—for instance, one mix for broadcast, another for live sound reinforcement, and yet another for recording.

- **Effects Channels**: Most advanced mixers include integrated effects processors, which can add reverb, delay, compression, and other audio effects directly within the mixer. This integration simplifies workflows and allows for real-time audio enhancement during live productions.

- **Digital Integration**: Digital mixers offer seamless integration with computer-based audio systems, providing not only audio routing and processing but also digital audio workstation (DAW) control. This integration is crucial for remote productions where audio signals might be managed across distributed locations, necessitating precise control and synchronization.

Choosing an Audio Mixer

The size and complexity of the production are key factors in selecting a mixer. Larger productions with multiple audio sources will require a mixer with more inputs and advanced routing capabilities. Conversely, a smaller production might only need a basic mixer with fewer inputs and features. In some cases, you may only require a virtual mixer because your audio sources are being sent directly to the cloud. For remote productions, particularly those that involve outdoor or on-location shoots, the portability and durability of the mixer are important. Compact, rugged mixers are ideal for such environments.

Remotely controlling hardware audio mixers

Hardware audio mixers such as the Presonus StudioLive III, are starting to come with built-in remote audio mixing services. PreSonus Metro is a new tool that enables high-quality, low-latency audio mixing over the Internet. Designed to integrate seamlessly with StudioLive Series III mixers, Metro allows users from anywhere in the world to connect and control the mixer remotely using the UC Surface interface. This allows you to connect multiple XLR and ¼" audio inputs into a single network connected audio mixer for remote production. The remote connectivity is facilitated through a secure peer-to-peer connection established via MyPreSonus account integration, ensuring both reliability and security during remote operations. Metro's capabilities extend across various applications, making it invaluable for a range of audio production scenarios. For instance, broadcasters can remotely create a broadcast mix from their homes, eliminating the need to be physically present at live events.

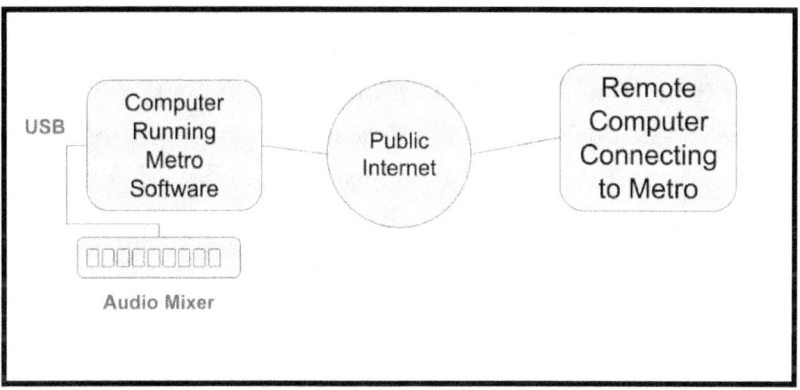

Simplified layout of Metro software connection to a remote location.

Troubleshooting and maintenance of StudioLive Series III mixers are also streamlined with Metro, so audio engineers can address and resolve mixer issues from their homes or offices without traveling to the site. This capability is crucial for maintaining the integrity and quality of live audio outputs without interruptions.

In contexts like corporate conferences, Metro offers the unique advantage of mixing audio for all-day events remotely. Metro also provides templates or starting points for less experienced audio engineers. This not only helps in elevating the overall audio quality but also in mentoring emerging professionals in the field.

Audio mixers are indispensable in the production of high-quality broadcast content. The choice of an audio mixer can profoundly impact the production's overall quality, making it essential to select a mixer that aligns with the specific needs of the environment and the goals of the production. You may decide to go with a software-only audio mixing solution as discussed in the previous chapter, or you may find it easier to use a remote production ready audio mixer such as the Presonus StudioLive III series. Broadcast professionals now have a wide array of possibilities for remote audio production.

KEY TAKEAWAYS FROM THIS CHAPTER:

1. **Hardware Integration in Remote Production**: The chapter emphasizes how PTZ cameras, encoders, decoders, controllers, networking equipment, and audio mixers form the backbone of remote production, each playing a pivotal role in capturing, processing, and transmitting content across various production workflows.

2. **Enhancing Flexibility and Scalability**: Advances in PTZ cameras, such as PoE support and NDI technology, provide versatile control and high-quality output. The seamless integration with cloud-based management allows broadcasters to quickly adjust and scale for dynamic production environments.

3. **Centralized Management Solutions**: Tools like Magewell Cloud, Kiloview's KiloLink Server, and Matrox ORIGIN streamline encoding and decoding by offering centralized management software. These platforms efficiently convert and manage streams between various protocols, enhancing the flexibility of broadcast workflows.

4. **Optimized Network Infrastructure**: Networking equipment like routers, switches, and modems ensure reliable data transmission. Netgear Pro AV switches, especially the M4250 series, cater to AV over IP workflows and simplify NDI integration, crucial for maintaining

robust network setups.

5. **Advanced Audio Mixer Control**: Modern audio mixers offer multi-bus mixing, effects channels, and digital integration. Remote-ready mixers, such as Presonus StudioLive III with its Metro tool, enable high-quality, low-latency audio management and control across distributed locations, ensuring reliable, professional-grade audio output.

15 CHALLENGES AND SOLUTIONS IN REMOTE PRODUCTION

Remote production has a unique set of challenges that can impact the quality and efficiency of productions. Understanding these challenges is crucial for developing effective strategies to overcome them and ensure successful remote production operations.

In remote production, challenges can arise at any stage—from initial setup and live broadcasting to post-production and distribution. For example, the venue may provide internet access which tests fine during your pre-production walkthrough and then during the event hundreds of smartphones start using the same WiFi connection. These issues can affect technical aspects, such as video and audio quality, as well as organizational dynamics, including team collaboration and workflow management. Addressing these challenges as early in the process as possible (i.e. during the site survey) is essential not only to maintain the high standards expected in professional broadcasts but also to leverage the full potential of remote production capabilities.

Bandwidth Issues

In remote production, several bandwidth-related challenges can significantly impact the quality and reliability of broadcasts. Network congestion, as mentioned above, often, leads to dropped frames and increased latency. You can avoid network congestion by setting up your own private network and using a VLAN (Virtual LAN) for your highest priority video and audio sources. Inadequate upload speeds are a critical issue, especially for uploading large video files or streaming high-quality video, resulting in poor stream quality and interruptions. Network bonding solutions or services such as Speedify allow you to create a stronger overall internet connection by bonding together sources such as hardwired ethernet, WiFi and cellular connections (even from multiple cellular networks). Speedify can help reduce unreliable internet connections which can fluctuate or drop intermittently, disrupting live broadcasts and affecting team collaboration. Bonding solutions can also help reduce the risk of bandwidth throttling by internet providers during high usage periods can unexpectedly reduce bandwidth availability, impacting both live and post-production workflows.

Additionally, latency can delay audio and video streams, crucially affecting live event timing and synchronization. Variable bitrate streaming may seem like a good idea in low-bandwidth environments but the variability can introduce latency between sources. Consider using constant bitrate connections for each IP-connected device.

Remote Production Tip for Troubleshooting IP Video Latency and Synchronizing Multiple IP Video Sources

When dealing with multiple IP cameras in a remote production setting, it's crucial to synchronize the video feeds and audio to avoid discrepancies that can detract from the professionalism of the stream. A solution to this involves using a common Network Time Protocol (NTP) server to ensure all devices, including cameras and PCs, are properly synchronized without introducing additional latency.

To begin, identify and select a Network Time Server that corresponds with your network equipment or is geographically close to your location to minimize latency. For example, a production based in Philadelphia might choose a server in New York or Virginia. After selecting a server, configure each camera through its web interface by setting the NTP settings under the "Network" section, adjusting the time zone, enabling NTP Time Sync, and specifying the server address and time interval.

Similarly, for PCs, whether Windows or Mac, adjust the system's time settings to synchronize with the same Network Time Server. This ensures that all video feeds from the cameras are synchronized to within 30 ms as tested, significantly reducing the chances of video latency and ensuring smooth, synchronous playback.

If audio synchronization is also required, simply route the audio output through the line-level input on the cameras to align the audio feed with the video feeds.

This method not only streamlines the synchronization of video and audio across multiple sources but also mitigates potential timing discrepancies between devices, ensuring a coherent and synchronized production output.

To address these challenges effectively, it is essential to engage in careful planning and implement contingency measures such as securing backup internet connections, using dedicated lines, and dynamically adjusting broadcast quality based on real-time bandwidth assessments. These strategies help maintain consistent broadcast quality and ensure that remote productions meet professional standards and fully leverage modern broadcasting technology.

Strategic Approaches to Overcoming Challenges in Remote Production

Successfully navigating the complexities of remote production requires not only addressing immediate technical and organizational issues but also adopting strategic approaches that leverage industry standards and emerging technologies. This section explores how adopting standards and integrating new technologies can provide robust solutions to the challenges faced in remote production.

The journey through the challenges and solutions in remote production underscores the importance of resilience and adaptability in the media sector. By understanding and addressing the complexities associated with remote production, teams can harness its full potential to produce engaging, high-quality content that meets the demands of modern audiences. The strategic adoption of new technologies and continual improvement of processes will ensure that remote production remains a vital and effective approach in the ever-evolving landscape of broadcast media.

16 Advanced Topics in Remote Production

Remote production has become increasingly prevalent in the media and broadcast industry, driven by advancements in technology and the need for more flexible content creation methodologies. While this shift offers numerous benefits, such as cost reduction and the ability to produce content from virtually anywhere, it also introduces a set of unique challenges that can impact the quality and efficiency of productions. Understanding these challenges is crucial for developing effective strategies to overcome them and ensure successful remote production operations.

More on SMPTE 2110

SMPTE 2110 is designed for high-end, large-scale productions and provides superior video quality. It separates video, audio, and ancillary data into different streams for easier management and supports PTP synchronization, ensuring precise timing across devices.

Choosing Between NDI and SMPTE 2110

The choice between NDI and SMPTE 2110 depends on specific production requirements, resources, and scale. NDI is ideal for productions where simplicity and cost are critical, making it a good choice for smaller production houses or those new to IP-based workflows. SMPTE 2110 is suited for environments that demand the highest quality and control, typical in professional broadcasting and large-scale events.

Many organizations may find benefits in using both standards, leveraging NDI for simpler tasks and SMPTE 2110 for projects requiring high fidelity and precise synchronization. Both NDI and SMPTE 2110 offer valuable features tailored to different needs within the video production industry. By understanding the capabilities and limitations of each, you can choose the most appropriate technology or combination of technologies to meet the specific demands of your projects.

More on Dante AV

Dante supports several video standards for flexible use cases including Dante AV Ultra, Dante AV-A and Dante AV-H. The Dante Controller is used for configuring and routing both audio and video devices with ease. Dante's solutions can operate on standard 1 GbE network infrastructure. That being said, each Dante video source will require additional bandwidth as you add them to your network. For example, each Dante AV Ultra source requires 700 Mbps while Dante AV-H requires only 30 Mbps.

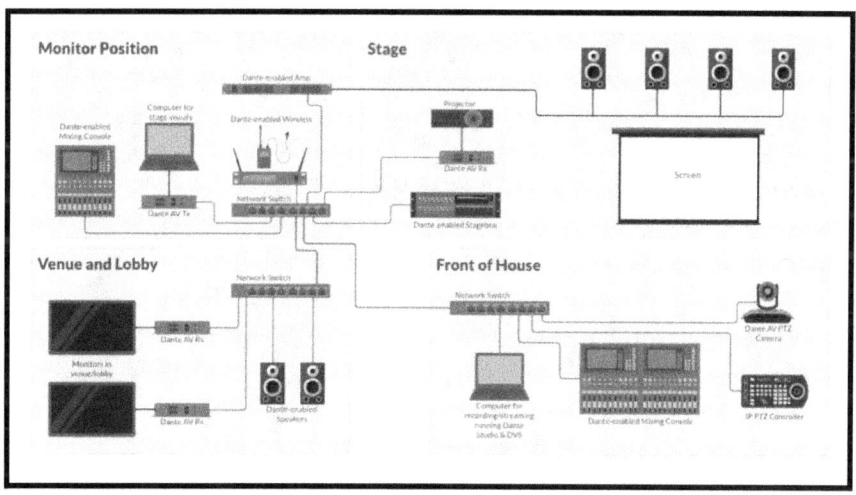

Dante AV networking setup for live events.

Feature	Dante AV Ultra	Dante AV-A	Dante AV-H

Resolution Support	Up to 4Kp60 4:4:4	Up to 4Kp60 4:4:4	Up to 4Kp60 4:2:0
Latency	Sub Frame	Sub Frame	A Few Frames
Interoperability of products using the same codec	Yes	Yes	Yes
Dante Controller Support	Yes	Yes	Yes
Dante Domain Manager and Dante Director Support	Yes	No	Yes
Dante Studio Software Support	Yes	No	Yes
HDCP Support	Yes	Yes	No
Common AV Clock	Yes	No	No
Encode/Decode from SDI	Yes	No	No

Several important Dante tools include Dante Studio, which can convert Dante video into a virtual webcam, making it easy to incorporate video flows into various applications and platforms. Users can integrate Dante enabled PTZ cameras and sources into video meeting platforms such as Teams and Zoom, capture video content for CMS platforms like Panopto, and add video streaming or recording to live events using software like OBS or vMix. This expansion into video provides simplified system maintenance and security is managed through Dante Domain Manager and Dante Director.

Advanced IP Audio Tools for Remote Production:

AES67 is an important standard in the world of networked audio, and its implementation in remote productions plays a significant role in enhancing audio management across various broadcast scenarios. AES67 is a standard for audio over IP and interoperability between different networked audio systems, which allows for high-quality audio streaming over IP networks. Here's a detailed look at AES67 and how it integrates into remote production environments:

What is AES67?

AES67 is an open standard for audio over IP and interoperability among various proprietary standards. It was developed by the Audio Engineering Society (AES) to enable high-performance audio networking between devices and systems that previously could not communicate due to differing underlying technologies. AES67 focuses on ensuring that various audio-over-IP systems can share audio streams across a network, even if they are built on different protocols such as Dante, Ravenna, or Q-LAN.

Dante for Remote Audio Production

Dante (Digital Audio Network Through Ethernet) is a network audio protocol that allows for multiple uncompressed audio channels to be transmitted across a standard Ethernet network. It is highly valued in remote productions for its low-latency, high-resolution audio transfer capabilities. Dante enables complex audio setups to be simplified through a virtual mixing environment, where audio from various remote locations can be managed and mixed without physical proximity constraints. Its ability to integrate seamlessly with existing network infrastructures makes it an optimal solution for live event productions, broadcast environments, and multi-site venues.

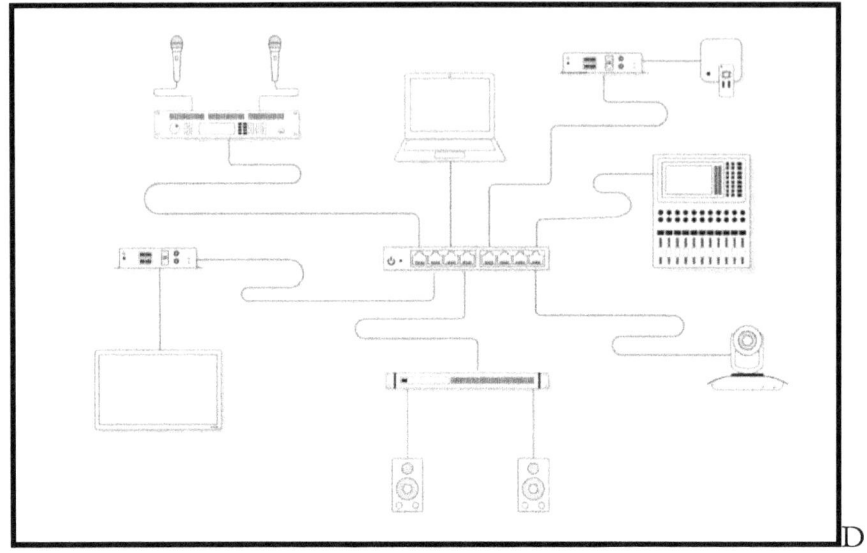

Dante network diagram.

Dante Connect enhances remote production by delivering synchronized audio from on-site Dante networks directly to cloud services. This integration allows for a more efficient use of personnel and hardware on the ground. By centralizing audio production in the cloud, broadcasters can significantly reduce costs and streamline their workflows. The use of Dante-enabled AV-over-IP devices ensures reliable and high-quality audio transmission, making Dante Connect an ideal solution for modern broadcasting environments that require flexibility and scalability.

Dante Director is a cloud-based software as a service (SaaS) application that facilitates the organization and management of Dante devices into logical groups. It allows for enhanced user access management, device security, and remote management of one or more Dante networks. This tool is crucial for maintaining control over complex audio setups across distributed locations.

Dante Controller routes AV signals between all Dante-enabled devices on a network. It saves configurations directly to the devices, ensuring network stability through power cycles, device disconnections, and system reconfigurations. This robust management tool is essential for maintaining seamless audio flows and ensuring high reliability in live production settings.

Bridging Dante and AES67:

Dante and AES67 can work in tandem, leveraging Dante's robust network management and low-latency capabilities alongside AES67's emphasis on interoperability across different audio networking platforms. This combination enables a more flexible and comprehensive audio networking system.

1. Use AES67 as an interoperability tool: AES67 can serve as a bridge in a Dante-dominated environment, allowing devices that are primarily configured for other protocols to communicate and integrate seamlessly with Dante-enabled devices.

2. Configure network settings appropriately: When integrating Dante and AES67, ensure that the network settings, such as synchronization and audio sample rates, are aligned across devices to maintain audio integrity and minimize latency.

3. Employ Dante Controller for management: utilize Dante Controller to manage Dante devices and configure AES67 streams within the Dante network. This approach harnesses Dante's ease of configuration and network stability while accommodating AES67 devices.

By understanding and deploying both Dante and AES67 according to their strengths—Dante for its network management and latency advantages, and AES67 for its interoperability—you can create a versatile and efficient audio network that accommodates a wide range of devices and protocols. This strategy ultimately enhances the capability and flexibility of audio networking systems in various professional settings.

Network Device Interface (NDI) for Audio:

For audio, NDI supports multi-channel, low-latency digital audio which can be routed independently of video, giving broadcasters flexible control over audio streams. This capability is crucial for remote productions where audio sources may not be physically close to the video sources or the production switcher. NDI Bridge can be used to send audio and video over the WAN from one LAN to another — as though they were on a single local area network.

NDI Audio Direct consists of a series of plugins that enable audio software applications to fully integrate with NDI-enabled networks. It allows these applications to send, receive, and manage multichannel audio streams with high fidelity and minimal latency. This capability is crucial for modern production environments where seamless audio integration across diverse software and hardware ecosystems is necessary.

More on Remote Audio Production

SourceConnect remains a favorite among audio professionals, known for its ultra-low latency streaming and ability to record and monitor simultaneously. It works with any digital audio workstation (DAW) and allows for multi-track recording across multiple time zones, making it ideal for high-quality, synchronous audio workflows. Audiomovers Listento is another powerful tool, offering high-resolution audio (32 bit/96 kHz) and support for multiple audio channels, including mono, stereo, quad, and surround sound. Its built-in recorder and user-selectable latencies make it perfect for ADR (automatic dialogue replacement) sessions that demand detailed audio production.

Source-Connect operates on a license basis, available either through purchase or monthly subscription, and it's considered the industry standard compared to alternatives like ipDTL, CleanFeed, and Zencastr. The standard version of Source-Connect meets the needs of most voice actors, though other paid and a free version, Source-Connect Now, are available. However, professional use typically requires a paid version as stipulated by agencies and clients.

Remote Production

SonoBus interface used for remote audio production.

SonoBus is an innovative application designed to streamline the process of streaming high-quality, low-latency audio between devices, whether over the internet or on a local network. This versatile tool stands out due to its ease of use and robust functionality, making it an excellent choice for audio professionals, musicians, and anyone needing to manage audio across different devices and platforms.

One of the most significant advantages of SonoBus is its ability to deliver peer-to-peer audio streaming with minimal latency. This feature is particularly valuable for live performances, rehearsals, and remote recording sessions, where real-time collaboration is essential, and delays can disrupt the flow of interaction.

SonoBus supports uncompressed PCM audio, ensuring that the audio quality remains pristine and lossless throughout the transmission. This capability is crucial for audio professionals and enthusiasts who require the highest fidelity in their projects.

The application interface takes some getting used to but it's ultimately well laid out based on the features it offers. Users can easily connect multiple devices across different operating systems, including Mac, Windows, iOS, and Android. This cross-platform compatibility can be useful if you are remotely producing audio and would like to connect additional sources to the mix.

SonoBus is completely free, making it an accessible option for individuals and organizations who might otherwise be unable to afford similar high-quality audio streaming solutions. SonoBus users can stream audio directly into most digital audio workstation (DAW) software.

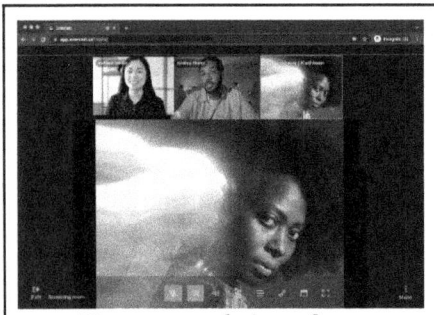
Evercast web-interface.

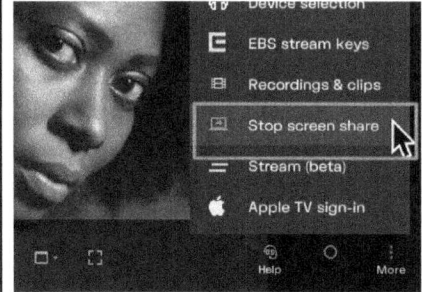
Evercast features.

Evercast is a real-time collaboration platform designed specifically for creatives involved in video production. It integrates video conferencing, HD live-streaming, and high-quality audio into a single web-based platform, making it convenient for various stages of production. The platform allows teams to share their creative workflows with ultra-low latency and high-quality output. This includes live cameras on set, as well as software like Avid, Premiere, Maya, and Pro Tools. Evercast's design focuses on enhancing creative collaboration, simulating an environment where team members are working together in the same space.

Bringing together remote audio and video sources, enable professionals to conduct live shows, recording sessions, and collaborative projects with high efficiency and quality. In an upcoming chapter, you will learn about hardware audio mixers that support remote mixing of physical XLR and ¼" audio inputs. Understanding your software and hardware options for remote audio production will allow you to choose the best solution for your next project.

Video Switchers in the Cloud

Live video switching is integral to remote production, enabling directors to select and switch between different video feeds in real time. Switchers can be either hardware-based or software-based. Software video switchings are increasingly utilized in remote production for their flexibility and scalability. The adoption of software-based switchers is particularly advantageous in remote settings where you want to leverage the cloud.

Earlier in the book, V2Cloud was mentioned as an easy way to deploy OBS software in the cloud. You can also deploy vMix in the cloud as well following vMix's published guidelines. To virtualize vMix and other similar software in the cloud effectively you can follow the following steps.

vMix Cloud Setup Requirements:

1. **Server Instance:** Utilize a Windows Server 2019 x64, allocating at least 4 CPU cores to handle the demands of live production.
2. **Graphics and Display:** It's crucial to have directly attached graphics with virtual display support, often available via technologies like NVIDIA Grid or NVIDIA Workstation Graphics. For Amazon EC2, instances labeled "G4" or higher are suitable.
3. **Drivers:** Only NVIDIA Grid drivers are compatible, and they must be installed as per Amazon EC2's guidance. Regular NVIDIA drivers are insufficient for this setup.

4. **Remote Access**: Avoid using Remote Desktop (RDP) for managing vMix. Options like VNC, Splashtop, TeamViewer and AnyDesk, or cloud-based desktop solutions like Teradici (which might involve additional costs) are recommended for optimal performance.

5. **Display Configuration**: Ensure the graphics card-connected display is set as the primary within Windows settings. All other monitors, especially those connected to a "Microsoft Basic Adapter," should be disabled to prevent conflicts.

Testing the Setup:

- Launch vMix and add an MP4 video file as input to check the graphics configuration. Proper display of the MP4 file indicates a successful setup, whereas issues in displaying the file could signal a misconfiguration in accessing the graphics card.

Benefits of Virtualizing vMix in the Cloud:

1. **Scalability and Flexibility**: Cloud instances can be scaled up or down based on the production requirements, providing flexibility in resource management.

2. **Accessibility**: Producers and directors can access the production setup from anywhere, reducing the need for physical infrastructure.

3. **Cost Efficiency**: Reduces the overhead costs associated with physical hardware and minimizes the maintenance expenses.

4. **Reliability**: Cloud platforms often offer high uptime and reliability compared to physical servers, which is critical for live production environments.

It's crucial to thoroughly test the entire setup in a cloud environment to ensure that it meets the demands of your production, especially since cloud services can be shared and might not always guarantee consistent performance. This setup process, when properly managed, can significantly enhance the flexibility and scalability of remote video production workflows.

WHIP (WebRTC-HTTP Ingest Protocol) and WebRTC (Web Real-Time Communication)

The integration of WHIP and WebRTC into remote production setups brings a host of benefits, particularly by addressing the long-standing issue of latency in live broadcasts. WHIP (WebRTC-HTTP Ingest Protocol) and WebRTC (Web Real-Time Communication) technologies allow for the delivery of audio and video content in real-time with minimal delay. This is crucial in remote production where the synchronicity and immediacy of feeds directly influence the quality of interaction and engagement during live events.

For producers and broadcasters, the ability to stream high-quality content with low latency means improved coordination among production teams, more dynamic interactions with live audiences, and the capacity to manage multiple feeds smoothly without the traditional delays that can detract from the viewing experience. These technologies not only enhance the viewer's experience by providing smoother, more immediate content but also empower producers to execute more complex and interactive live events.

Furthermore, the availability of these technologies in OBS Studio 30.0, a leading free and open-source software for video recording and live streaming, democratizes high-quality production capabilities. With OBS 30, users now have access to WHIP and WebRTC support, allowing them to experiment with and deploy these advanced technologies in their productions at no additional cost. This inclusion in OBS 30 opens up possibilities for creators of all levels to explore innovative broadcasting techniques and improve their production workflows using the latest advancements in streaming technology.

17 THE FUTURE OF BROADCASTING

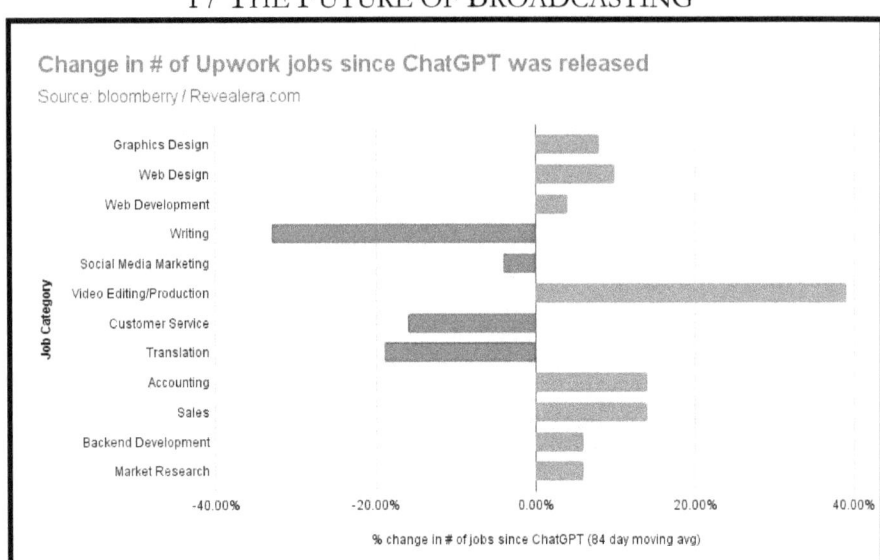

Image from Seer Interactive.

There has been huge growth in video editing and production demand in 2024 as shown with change in jobs posted on Upwork since the release of ChatGPT. The graph above shows a trend many of us have noticed in the live streaming and video production industry. Since the release of ChatGPT, it has become easier to create a video advertising plan and execute with an AI assistant. With a 40% increase in video production job demand it's almost as if ChatGPT is recommending video campaigns to millions of users who are asking questions like "How can I grow my business in 2024?"

When I posted this question on LinkedIn, many of my peers in the industry have responded with caution and worry about the new AI video production tools that are hitting the market. One of particular interest, SORA, OpenAIs new text to video generation tool, claims that it can make "stunning" videos from a simple text prompt. If SORA is anything like ChatGPT, the industry is going to be in for some significant change. Is the temporary boost in video production going to maintain its significant growth or will it decline like other job categories such as writing and social media marketing?

One area of interest to our team is live video production. I wholeheartly believe live video content will continue to increase in value as AI video becomes more prevalent. This is because the value of "authentic" real-time video communication will increase as a result of so much "lost personal touch" with AI generated video.

he StreamGeeks Live Streaming Studio integrated with Zoom.

From my vantage point at StreamGeeks, I've observed AI's role in automating processes like video editing, a domain once heavily reliant on human expertise. Photorealistic AI-generated videos arenare already emerging. The duality of AI – as a powerful assistant and a potential replacement – is something we can't ignore. It's fascinating, for instance, how AI can streamline tasks such as tracking PTZ camera movements, providing transcriptions and enhancing the efficiency and creative possibilities of live streaming.

As someone working in the world of live streaming and video production, I see this as a pivotal moment. The industry stands at a crossroads where AI-generated content and the authenticity of human creativity are in a delicate balance. This isn't just about technology overtaking tasks; it's about redefining how we position ourselves for "productivity gains" to compete in this modern landscape.

The future of video production will likely revolve around a synergy between human creativity and AI's efficiency. But how far will we need to pivot our skills towards areas where AI can't replicate the nuanced understanding and creative insights we bring to the table. Learning to manage and work alongside AI, understanding its capabilities and limitations, will be crucial. We need to be the conductors of this technological orchestra, blending AI's computational power with our irreplaceable creative spirit.

It's great that we are seeing a temporary boom in the demand for video production but I think we are all wondering how far can AI transform the industry? A second wave of specialty-AI video production tools are on their way to being released. My message to fellow video production professionals is one of optimism and resilience. Let's embrace this change, continue to learn, and find ways to complement our skills with AI advancements. The future isn't about AI versus humans; it's about how we can harmonize these forces to create content that resonates with authenticity and innovation.

Technological Advances

The future of remote production is likely to be dominated by continued advancements in artificial intelligence (AI), 5G connectivity, and next-generation streaming protocols. AI is expected to increasingly automate complex production tasks, such as video editing and camera operations, reducing the need for manual intervention and allowing for more sophisticated content creation. This automation will also aid in managing large datasets and streams, ensuring that the production can adapt in real-time to changing inputs and conditions.

5G technology will drastically enhance remote production capabilities through its ultra-fast speeds and incredibly low latency. This will facilitate more reliable and high-quality live broadcasts from remote locations and enable the use of more mobile devices and sensors in production, thereby increasing the flexibility and scope of broadcasting projects.

Globalization of Production

Remote production technologies will also continue to break down geographical barriers, enabling truly global production teams. This globalization will allow producers to select the best talent from around the world, regardless of location. Collaboration across different time zones and regions will become smoother and more efficient, enabled by cloud-based tools and platforms that support real-time communication and file sharing.

This global network of production resources will not only enhance the diversity and quality of content but will also allow for more localized and culturally relevant content to be produced on a global scale.

The evolution of remote production is set on a trajectory that promises to reshape the broadcasting landscape dramatically. With technological advances in AI, 5G, and IP-based workflows, coupled with the integration of media technologies and the globalization of production teams, the future of broadcasting looks bright. These developments will enable broadcasters to create more engaging, high-quality, and diverse content more efficiently than ever before. As the industry moves forward, embracing these changes will be key to staying competitive and relevant in the rapidly evolving media world.

Thank you for journeying through the pages of this book. You have now reached the end, but let this not be the conclusion of your learning or your exploration in the dynamic field of remote production. You are poised at the threshold of limitless possibilities, equipped with the knowledge and tools to elevate your projects and take remote production to unprecedented heights.

As you apply the insights and techniques discussed, remember that innovation thrives on collaboration and sharing. We invite you to join the StreamGeeks community—a vibrant network of enthusiasts and professionals who are passionate about streaming and content creation. Your unique experiences, challenges, and successes can inspire and enlighten others, just as you might find inspiration and guidance in the journeys of your peers.

Embrace the opportunity to transform the landscape of media production, to innovate and to lead in crafting engaging, high-quality remote productions. The future of media is not just in the technology we use but in the communities we build and the stories we share. Let your journey be bold, let your streams shine bright, and always remember—the StreamGeeks community is here to support you every step of the way.

You can stay connected with our latest updates by signing up for our StreamGeeks Newsletter we send out each month. You can sign up at StreamGeeks.us/newsletter.

Further Reading

To enhance your understanding and expertise in remote production, several additional resources are available that delve deeper into specific tools and technologies. Each of these works provides valuable insights and practical guidance that are pivotal for anyone looking to advance their knowledge in the field of remote media production:

1. *The Basics of Live Streaming:* This book reviews the major aspects of live streaming and explores each area with simple language. It's important to understand the fundamentals before you jump into more complicated topics. This book is a great way to bring new hires up to speed.

2. *The Unofficial Guide to vMix*: This guide is an essential resource for users of vMix, a software that allows for live video production, including mixing, switching, and streaming. The book covers a comprehensive range of functionalities from basic setup to advanced features like instant replay and stinger transitions, making it invaluable for producing high-quality live events remotely.

3. *The Unofficial Guide to NDI*: Network Device Interface (NDI) is a crucial technology for transmitting video over a network with minimal latency, which is fundamental in remote production environments. This guide provides a detailed look at the setup, integration, and troubleshooting of NDI systems, offering practical

advice for optimizing your workflow in distributed production settings.

4. *The OBS SuperUser Guidebook*: Open Broadcaster Software (OBS) is widely used for video recording and live streaming, with versatile capabilities suited to remote production. This guidebook serves as a deep dive into the advanced features of OBS, helping users maximize the software's potential in creating professional-grade live streams from various locations.

5. *The Virtual Ticket*: This book explores the concept of delivering engaging virtual experiences to audiences, which is a rapidly growing area within remote production. It offers strategies for monetizing digital events and enhancing viewer engagement, providing a blueprint for successfully navigating the digital event landscape.

6. *The PTZ Camera Operator Handbook*: The PTZ Camera Operator Handbook is an essential guide to robotic camera operations. The popularity of streaming video content – both creating and consuming it–is transforming many people into "amateur/expert" video producers. Whether it's streaming live video for events and community groups, work, school, sports, or home, more people are embracing video production.

Each of these texts offers a unique perspective and set of tools that can significantly benefit practitioners and enthusiasts of remote production, ensuring that readers are well-equipped to tackle the challenges and opportunities presented by remote and distributed production environments.

ABOUT THE AUTHOR

Paul Richards is a father, author, and business executive leading his company in the field of digital video communications. Richards is the author of multiple top-selling books including, "The Virtual Ticket," "The Online Meeting Survival Guide," and "Helping Your Church Live stream."

Richards' books draw on his hands-on experience in the multimedia technology industry. As the Director of Business Development for HuddleCamHD and PTZOptics, Richards is the host of multiple online shows that feature his work on YouTube, Facebook, LinkedIn, and Twitch.

Richards is also the Chief Streaming Officer at StreamGeeks and teaches Udemy courses online to over 50,000 registered students.

Course topics include live video production, online communications, and social media connectivity.

GLOSSARY OF TERMS

3.5mm Audio Cable: Often a male-to-male stereo cable, common in standard audio uses.

4K: A high definition resolution option (3840 x 2160 pixels or 4096 x 2160 pixels)

Application Program Interface (API): an (often) web-based interface between one or more software applications (including browsers) and another that allows commands to be sent that provide external (remote) control.

Bandwidth - The range of frequencies within a given band that are used for transmitting a signal.

Broadcasting - The distribution of audio or video content to a dispersed audience via any electronic mass communications medium.

Broadcast Frame Rates - Used to describe how many frames per second are captured in broadcasting. Common frame rates in broadcast video include: **29.97fps and 59.94 fps.**

Capture Card - A device with inputs (and often outputs) that allows cameras and other video sources (and destinations) to connect to a computer.

Chroma Key - A video effect that replaces a color in the scene (usually a background color like blue or green) with other video content
Cloud-Based Streaming - Streaming and video production interaction that occurs within the cloud and is therefore accessible beyond a single user's computer device.

Color Matching - The process of managing color and luminance settings on multiple cameras to match their appearance.

Community Strategy - The strategy of building one's brand and product recognition by building meaningful relationships with an audience, partner, and client base.

Content Delivery Network (CDN) - A network of servers that delivers web-based content to an end user.

CPU (Central Processing Unit) - The electronic component within a computer that carries out the instructions of a computer program by performing the basic arithmetic, logical, control, and input/output (I/O) operations specified by the instructions.

DAW - Digital Audio Workstation.

DB9 Cable - A common cable connection for camera joystick serial control.

Dynamic Host Configuration Protocol (DHCP) Router - A router with a network management protocol that dynamically sets IP addresses so the server can communicate with its sources.

Encoder - A device or software that converts a piece of code or info to then distribute it.

H.264 & H.265 - Common formats of video recording, compression, and delivery.

High Definition Multimedia Interface (HDMI) - A cable commonly used for transmitting audio/video.

High Efficiency Video Coding (HEVC) - H.265, one of the most common formats of video, MJPEG-H Part 2.

Internet Protocol (IP) Camera/Video - A camera or video source that can send and receive information via a network & internet.

IP Control - The ability to control/connect a camera or device via a network or internet.

Latency - The time it takes between sending a signal and the recipient receiving it; usually measured in milliseconds (ms)

Live Streaming - The process of sending and receiving audio and or video over the internet.

Local Area Network (LAN) - A network of computers linked together in one location.

Multicorder - A feature of Vmix and some other streaming software that allows the user to record raw footage or multiple camera feeds to separate files from the stream output.

Network Device Interface (NDI®) - A software standard developed by NewTek to enable video-compatible products to communicate, deliver, and receive broadcast quality video in a high quality, low latency manner that is frame-accurate and suitable for switching in a live production environment.

NDI® Camera - A camera that allows you to send and receive video over your LAN.

NDI® | HX - NDI® High Efficiency, optimizes NDI® for limited bandwidth environments.

Network - A digital telecommunications infrastructure which allows nodes to share resources. In computer networks, computing devices exchange data with each other using connections between nodes.

NTSC - Video standard used in North and South America, Japan, and the Caribbean. It's also used in some other countries,

OTT Streaming (Over-The-Top) - When a content creator or media service bypasses typical cable media outlets (often called "walled gardens") and goes "over-the-top" (or the wall) to distribute content through other means (ie. Facebook, YouTube, Twitch)

PAL - Analog video format widely used outside of North America.

PCIe Card - Connects to a computer's motherboard or external enclosure to enable high bandwidth communication between an internal or external device (i.e. a graphics or video capture card) and the computer

PoE (also PoE+ and PoE++) - Power over ethernet (and higher wattage versions)

PTZ - Pan, tilt, zoom.

RS-232 - Serial camera control transmission.

Real Time Messaging Protocol (RTMP) - RTMP is a standard protocol for sending and receiving video to a server. RTMP is used to deliver video streams over the public internet to CDNs such as Facebook or YouTube.

Real Time Streaming Protocol (RTSP) - Network control protocol for streaming from point to point.

Additional Online Courses:

Join over 100,000 other students who are learning how to use the power of live streaming! Take the following courses taught by Paul Richards for free by downloading the course coupon codes available at streamgeeks.us/start.

- **Facebook Live Streaming** - *Beginner*

This course will take you through the basics of Facebook Live. The course has been updated twice and includes instructions for using Facebook Live Reactions.

- **YouTube Live Streaming** - *Beginner*

This course covers the basics of YouTube Live.. It also includes essential branding and marketing tips.

- **Introduction to OBS (Open Broadcaster Software)**

This course covers one of the world's most popular FREE live streaming software solutions. OBS is a great place to start live streaming for free.

- **Introduction to xSplit Software** - *Beginner*

This course takes you through xSplit which has more features than OBS but costs roughly $5/month. Learn how to create impressive live productions and make your videos much faster with xSplit.

- **Introduction to vMix** - *Intermediate*

The vMix Windows-based software tool will have you live streaming like the pros in no time.

- **Introduction to Wirecast** - *Intermediate*

Wirecast is the preferred software for many professional live streamers and is available for Mac and PC.

- **Introduction to NewTek NDI®** - *Intermediate*

NewTek's innovative IP video standard NDI® (Network Device Interface) will change the way you think about live video production. Learn how to use this innovative new technology for live streaming and video production system design.

- **Introduction to Live streaming course** - *Beginner*

This course includes everything you need to start designing your show like a starter pack of course files including Photoshop, After Effects, and free Virtual Sets.

- **Introduction to Live streaming** - *Intermediate*

This course focuses on more advanced techniques for optimizing your production workflow and using compression to get the most out of your processor. This course includes files for Photoshop, After Effects, and free Virtual Sets.

- **Helping Your Church Live Stream** - *Intermediate*

This course focuses on live streaming for churches and houses of worship. We tackle some of the specific challenges about live streaming in a house of worship.

- **How to Live stream A Wedding** - *Beginner*

This is a great course for anyone looking to start live streaming weddings. It was originally designed for wedding photographers to add a live streaming service to their existing portfolio of offerings.

www.ingramcontent.com/pod-product-compliance
Lightning Source LLC
Chambersburg PA
CBHW052148220526
45471CB00004B/1574